Anyone Can Swim

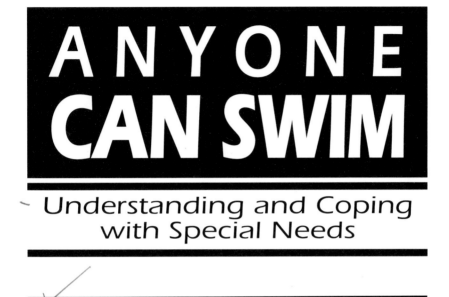

ANYONE CAN SWIM

Understanding and Coping with Special Needs

Amateur Swimming Association
Edited by Joan A Harrison

The Crowood Press

First published in 1989 by
The Crowood Press
Ramsbury, Marlborough,
Wiltshire SN8 2HE

British Library Cataloguing in Publication Data

Anyone can swim: understanding and coping with special needs
1. Swimming, – Manuals
I. Harrison, Joan A. II. Amateur Swimming Association

ISBN 1 85223 144 0

Cover photograph by Tracy K. Johnson – National Union of
Townswomen's Guilds Regional Swimming Day (Bristol), sponsored by
the National Westminster Bank.

Typeset by Qualitext Typesetting, Abingdon, Oxon
Printed in Great Britain by The Bath Press

Contents

The Contributors:

John Decourcy – Development Assistant (rehabilitation) at Moray House College, Edinburgh.
Sheila Dobie – Moray House College, Edinburgh and an ASA Senior Staff Tutor.
Joan A. Harrison – Sunderland Polytechnic and an ASA Senior Staff Tutor. She is a member of the Northern Council for Sport and Recreation.
Valerie Lambert – West Hill College, Birmingham and an ASA Senior Staff Tutor.
Tony Mackenzie-Farmer – North East Worcestershire College and an ASA Senior Staff Tutor.
Alan R. Thornton – Co-ordinator of the National Association of Swimming Clubs for the Handicapped.

The contributors to this book are all actively involved in teaching children and adults with special needs, and in the training of teachers.

Acknowledgements

The editor extends her thanks to the following for their contributions to this publication:

Written Text:

Sheila Dobie and John Decourcy   Chapter 4
Valerie Lambert   Chapter 2
Tony Mackenzie-Farmer   Chapter 5
Alan Thornton   Chapter 8

Illustrations:

Audio Visual Aid Department of Moray House College of Education, Edinburgh   Chapter 4
Christine Hill   Other illustrations

Photographs:

Fig 57 reproduced by kind permission of the *Bromsgrove Advertiser*.

Thanks also to Norma Bailey for typing the manuscript, and to John Verrier for his advice.

Foreword

The material in this long overdue book is a culmination of the work and experience of practised, observant teachers. They have, over the years, developed experimental teaching methods and had the initiative to involve people with disabilities in valuable water activities. As people live longer, with higher expectations, and as medicine advances, it is plain that the teaching of swimming to those with special needs will continue to develop.

In an era of sport for all, the growth of parent and child aquatic activity classes and of swimming for adults reveal a public awareness of the value of involvement in health-related programmes.

Those with special needs share the same values, and their performances in achieving and enjoying traditional stroke patterns, in swimming distances, and in competitive events are outstanding.

With the expanding involvement in swimming of people with special needs there is a need for teachers of swimming, and their colleagues in recreation and leisure management, to extend their horizons. The philosophy and knowledge required are to be found in this timely work.

J.W. Verrier
Education Officer,
Amateur Swimming Association

Introduction

The Value of Water Activities

There are few other sports which provide the opportunity for enjoyable and worthwhile participation for such a wide range of the community as swimming. With few barriers to taking part, it is a lifelong activity and one which can include the whole family together. It is a sport that can be performed indoors or outdoors, as one of a group, as an individual, or in an organised club or class. It offers great variety, including recreational swimming, survival and life-saving skills, synchronised swimming, diving, water games, aqua-fit and competitive swimming. The ability to swim opens the door to participation in other water sports, such as canoeing, sailing, water skiing sailboarding, surfing and subaqua.

All swimmers, however competent, have at one time been nervous beginners frightened to launch out into the water, frightened to wet their faces. There are some people who require greater help to cope with this new and unusual environment because of their age, a deep-rooted sense of fear, some physical or sensory impairment, or because of their limited ability to learn. These people need expert teachers who can formulate appropriate objectives, use a variety of teaching methods to achieve results, and constantly evaluate the success of their programmes. This book aims to give guidance on facilities, teaching methods and skills and to help all teachers understand more fully the needs of these potential swimmers. As well as advising teachers, this book should help parents, friends, club leaders, baths staff, in fact all who are prepared to encourage somebody to enjoy movement in water. The book can be used as a basis for teaching swimming or as a self-help guide. Those who wish to begin to teach swimming after reading this book may need further information on swimming skills or on disabilities. For this reason I have included a section of further reading (*see* page 158).

The book is about having fun in the water, which will only happen if the learning environment and atmosphere are right. For those people severely restricted in movement or understanding, the opportunity to move in water may extend their horizon beyond their usual four walls or their dependence on a wheelchair. Movement in water offers independence and the opportunity is also there to become a helper in the water or in the administration of the club. To learn to swim is only a start to further opportunities.

Involvement in any sporting activity has many values, but for some people swimming will be the only source of free movement so it is important to consider what particular values may accrue. Teachers should consider these as long-term objectives, from which more immediately attainable objectives arise.

Water activities provide opportunities

for social, psychological and physical development. Swimming's uniqueness lies in its use of the buoyancy of the water as a support for the body. Sustained by the water, a normally handicapped person can perform otherwise impossible movements. Even those unable to walk or with very limited movement on land can move in water and learn to swim. Mentally retarded pupils find the buoyancy of the water comforting and calming, giving a sense of security and an opportunity to relax.

The support of the water can reduce the pressure of body weight on the legs or spine, enabling an upright posture to be attained without support, and without damage to affected parts. Water support minimises the effects of weak muscles and the lack of balance and stability that hinder or restrict movement out of the water. Those who have restricted movements in the joints caused by pain and stiffness benefit from the increased range of movement which can be achieved in water. This support also enables babies to play and move safely with great confidence.

As well as providing support to the body, water gives resistance to movement which helps in the physiological development of the body. This resistance is used to give propulsion in swimming and to give power to an aqua-fit programme. It is the water resistance that makes swimming one of the best forms of exercise and re-education for damaged joints or muscles.

Values and Objectives in Teaching Swimming

Psychological Values

(i) An appreciation of personal success, giving a sense of achievement.
(ii) An improvement in self-image and a development of independence.
(iii) A sense of physical well-being which may help confidence and poise.
(iv) An improvement in self-discipline.
(v) An opportunity for self-expression and creativity.
(vi) An opportunity to experience risk and challenge.

Physiological Values

The beneficial effects upon the body result from the amount and nature of the work performed in swimming. Even mild activity in the water has a good effect upon those whose movements are severely restricted. Recent research has pointed to the need for all people to engage in frequent appropriate exercise to maintain or improve a healthy lifestyle. This regular physical activity is essential for several reasons:

(i) To help normal growth and development of the skeletal system.
(ii) To improve the functions of the heart and cardiovascular system.
(iii) To improve stamina and functional capacity.
(iv) To promote muscle strength which is important for joint stability and good posture.
(v) To improve body awareness and kinaesthetic sense.
(vi) To develop co-ordination and perceptual motor-ability.

(vii)   To help in the maintenance of a desirable body weight.

(viii)   As therapy after injury to assist the rehabilitation process.

(ix)   Through an improvement in the general level of health, the learning of movement skills in water is facilitated.

Whilst an improvement in general health should accrue from swimming, there are important sociological values in swimming which may for some be the main reasons for joining a swimming class or club.

Sociological Values

The opportunity to swim may fulfil certain sociological needs, including:

(i)   The opportunity to participate with the family, with friends or with a community group.

(ii)   Integration into mainstream activities.

(iii)   The development of safety awareness in or near water.

(iv)   The opportunity to share responsibilities, to co-operate with others.

(v)   The opportunity to be involved in competition at appropriate levels.

(vi)   The exercise of qualities of leadership.

(vii)   The enhancement of communication skills.

(viii)   The acceptance of different roles and responsibilities, particularly by helping in the running of a club.

The Teacher's Role

Each person will swim for different reasons and will gain from it in different ways. The successful achievement of both general aims and more specific objectives depends mainly on the teacher, whose previous experience, preconceived ideas, methods of teaching, concern for individuals and ability to assess and to adapt will influence the educational and recreational experience.

True understanding on the part of the teacher or helper is one of the most essential factors influencing the success of a swimming pool programme. The teacher who has a special awareness of the needs of the pupils, and given this understanding is able to react appropriately, is likely to be successful. A teacher who lacks sensitivity will find work with people with special needs a restrictive and unrewarding labour. The teacher must be confident in the ability of the pupils and approach the task positively; teaching water activities to people with special needs is most rewarding.

For this book people with special needs are identified as:

- babies and toddlers
- persistent non-swimmers
- ethnic minority groups
- adults, particularly non-swimmers
- pre- and post-natal women
- people with physical and/or sensory disability
- people with learning difficulties

Chapters 1 to 4 consider facilities, teaching methods, swimming skills and handling applicable in some part to all groups. Chapters 5 to 8 relate to the special groups and individuals.

1 Facilities, Safety and Hygiene

One of the aims of swimming programmes for people with special needs should be equality of opportunity for participation which must include integrated provision. There are some disabled people who will always require special facilities; these may not necessarily be segregated facilities and in fact, wherever possible they should be shared. It has been found that the managers of sports centres are often uncertain about the needs of special swimming groups or of people with disability wishing to use the centre. More people with special needs would be likely to use sport and leisure centres if physical and programme access were more sensitively attuned to their requirements.

The success of any swimming programme depends to a certain degree on the adequate provision of appropriate facilities and of a safe environment. Teachers should familiarise themselves with the conditions necessary to accommodate the different needs of pupils. Good facilities should provide a comfortable and interesting environment which should be safe, hygienic and serve individual needs. No provision is ever ideal but problems can be avoided by an awareness of essential requirements. There will be some facilities provided primarily for people with disabilities which give a most suitable environment for parent and baby or adult non-swimming groups. Conversely, people with disability may be able to use their local community swimming pool if there is ease of access and if the management and pool staff are aware of their needs.

Generally there are few modifications that need to be made to meet the needs of special swimming groups. Creative solutions can very often be found to problems relating to accessibility, given the right attitude and desire to give equal opportunity for participation in aquatic activities. People with disabilities who wish to swim are often prepared to overcome many difficulties but the best facilities possible should be available for all users. Many of the requirements of swimmers with special needs will also benefit the able-bodied swimmer.

The ideal facility, considered in this chapter, is for use by all swimmers with special needs. For some groups there are very few additional requirements to the normal community pool.

The Ideal Facility

General Access

(i) Adequate provision for parking should be as near as possible to the entrance to the buildings, with spaces designated for disabled people's vehicles.
(ii) Footpaths and ramps should have a

minimum width of 1.2m (3ft 11in) for wheelchairs, and a width of 2m (6ft 6in) where chairs need to pass each other.

(iii)   Gradients should not exceed 1:12 (8%).

(iv)   Path and ramp surfaces should be firm, smooth and non-slip.

(v)   A long ramp should have one or more landings.

(vi)   Handrails should be provided.

(vii)   Steps should be of uniform depth and height, with distinctive contrasting treads and rises for the visually impaired.

(viii)   Directional signs should be clear for the visually handicapped, and the hearing-impaired who may be unable or hesitant to make enquiries.

(ix)   The entrance to the building should have a canopy to provide shelter.

(x)   Pools with an entrance turnstile should have a pass-gate to give access to wheelchair users.

(xi)   Reception areas should have plain glass to facilitate lip reading.

(xii)   The use of gratings or mat wells should be avoided as they are a potential hazard to the semi-ambulant.

(xiii)   Access should be provided to all areas via ramps or lifts.

(xiv)   Doors should be easy to open; lever handles are preferable to door knobs.

(xv)   Corridors should be no less than 1.2m (3ft 11in) wide, and projections which reduce this measurement should be avoided. Floor surfaces in contrasting colours should be used to indicate changes in floor level.

(xvi)   Smooth walls with handrails, and floors which are non-slip whether wet or dry, are important for safety in moving around.

(xvii)   Social amenities, such as cafeterias, spectator areas and suitably designed telephones and toilets should be accessible.

(xviii)   An amplified telephone should be provided for the hearing-impaired.

(xix)   Fire and emergency exits should cater for the needs of the non-ambulant.

Changing Facilities

Adequate time should always be allowed for changing, and ideal conditions should provide for those who are inevitably slower.

(i)   Changing facilities should be warm to maintain comfort when changing, which can be a slow and laborious process.

(ii)   There should be adequate space for those who need to manoeuvre a wheelchair or to lie horizontally to be changed.

(iii)   An open-plan design is best, with benches in addition to cubicles. Individual cubicles are preferred by certain ethnic groups and by many adults.

(iv)   A bench for the changing of severely disabled people will be needed, which should be 60cm (2ft) wide, 2m (6ft 6in) long and 50cm (20in) off the floor with a hinged edge which can be raised to prevent the person rolling inadvertently to the floor. The bench should be positioned to allow free access for wheelchairs. Benches are also needed for changing babies for water activities.

(v)   Lockers, for storing braces and corsets, should be 60cm (2ft)×60cm (2ft) and no more than 1.2m (3ft 11in) above the floor.

(vi)   Safe areas such as play pens enable a baby to play safely whilst a parent is changing.

(vii)   The changing room floor should slope slightly for drainage and should have a non-slip surface.

(viii) Changing and toileting cubicles should have at least the minimum dimensions to allow wheelchair access, and be provided with outward-opening doors. Vertical rails can be particularly useful for those who find difficulty in raising and lowering themselves.

(ix) Cubicles positioned near the shallow end of the pool can be an added advantage for those immobilised once callipers or similar aids are removed.

(x) Pre-cleansing and showering facilities should be accessible to all disabled, whether ambulant or using a shower chair.

(xi) Tap levers should be easy to operate, hair driers should be fitted with an extendable hose, and mirrors should be positioned at varying heights.

(xii) If the normal changing accommodation is entirely unsuitable for people with disabilities, ethnic groups or parent and baby groups, it may be possible to adapt staff or first aid rooms near to the poolside, or to make use of family changing units.

Access from the Changing Room to the Poolside

(i) Access areas should be non-slip and free from obstructions.

(ii) Showers should be without steps (where a footbath is by-passed, a disinfectant trough or mat should be available). Thermostats should be accurate and reliable.

(iii) Footbaths should be ramped or by-passed and fitted with handrails.

(iv) The distance from the changing room to the poolside should be as short as possible.

At the Poolside

(i) Handrails conforming to those leading from the changing rooms should be provided.

(ii) Warmed benches, 50cm (20in) high and 40cm (16in) wide, should be provided for the elderly or those who need frequent rests.

(iii) The poolside should be at least 1.5m (4ft 11in) to 2m (6ft 7in) wide with a clear space for wheelchairs. Care should be taken to ensure that wheelchairs do not carry dirt into the pool area.

(iv) A raised edge may pose problems when lifting heavy people into the water, and should be avoided.

(v) The poolside surface should be non-slip but care in use is required to avoid abrasions; a texture and colour contrast on the pool verge is useful.

Access to the Water

(i) Vertical steps should have generous footholds, and the accompanying rails must continue down to the pool bottom.

(ii) Gradually descending platform steps can be useful as they provide a useful play area for the timid child and give easy access for parents and babies, but they must be accompanied by rails, either centrally or at the sides.

(iii) Ramps can aid entry for the elderly and semi-ambulant and are useful particularly when shower chairs are available, but with both shallow steps and ramps a common problem is that of reduced pool space. This can be overcome by building the facility so that the descent is outside the actual pool area. Portable ramps, chutes and steps could also be constructed.

(iv) A slide can be fun, but it needs to

be positioned where there is a minimum depth of 1m (3ft 3in) at entry point and where the slide can be secured firmly on to the poolside.

(v) Projecting pool rails can be useful for independent entrances and exits.

(vi) Shower chairs, although they have small wheels, can be useful for taking swimmers to the poolside. As there are no brakes on these chairs their use must be carefully supervised.

(vii) A strong canvas seat with lifting handles on each side makes carrying safe and comfortable, and such an aid can be used to transfer someone directly into the water from a wheelchair.

(viii) A foam rubber pad or mattress placed on the poolside can offer insensitive limbs protection from abrasion.

(ix) Ground-level trolleys give the opportunity for self-propulsion for children who are non-ambulant.

(x) Fixed lifts and hoists are not generally required, but in special schools or hydrotherapy pools where there may be several swimmers with severe physical disabilities or heavy people, then mechanical hoists may be valuable. Whenever possible properly trained helpers should be used for entries and exits.

General Safety

Resting places are essential, and may take the form of rails, steps, platforms, and lane or width ropes. Rails are also useful for those who are unable to stand to recover and rest during a swim. Where a rail or steps are not present, a resting platform should be provided. Shallow steps can serve this purpose admirably, but lane or width ropes can also serve as supports for swimmers who are unable to stand and rest.

The pool bottom, which should be non-slip, should be marked with lines to warn of any sudden depth changes. Windows provide a pleasant, light atmosphere, but can create supervisory problems by casting reflections on the water. Curtains or blinds should be provided at windows to give privacy if required.

Water Temperature

A higher than normal temperature is desirable for those who are unable to be very active in the water. It assists relaxation and helps the pupil to concentrate on learning water skills. All the groups being considered in this book require a water temperature ranging ideally from 82–86°F (28–30°C). For the minority requiring higher temperatures, provision is more appropriately made in special schools or hydrotherapy pools. The relationship between water and air temperatures is a crucial factor; the air temperature must be higher than that of the water.

Types of Pool

Hydrotherapy Pools

These pools, often found in hospitals and schools, are designed specifically for rehabilitation purposes, in particular for the performance of therapy exercises selected by physiotherapists or hydrotherapists. The usual size of such a pool is approximately 6–8m (20–26ft) long and 3.5–4.5m (11–15ft) wide, the depth ranging from 85cm to 1.5m (33–59in). They may be 'deck-level' in design, which eases the process of entry and exit, but where therapists work from the pool-side, a 'raised edge pool' may be preferred to avoid a permanently crouched stance. The water temperature may range from 86–100°F (30–38°C). The air temperature should be higher than that of the water. Whenever the pool temperature is maintained at a high level, the rate of air change must be carefully regulated.

School Pools

Many schools for children with special needs are provided with a purpose-built pool. The size may vary from that of a hydrotherapy pool to that of a standard school swimming pool. The water temperature should be maintained at a level suitable for the needs of those using the pool. This can range from 82–92°F (28–34°C). A well-planned pool building will include specifically designed changing rooms and access areas, particularly into the water. A mechanical hoist is an added advantage. These pools are useful for parent and baby groups, adults and certain ethnic groups as they usually offer a warm and private facility.

Deck Level Pools

These are convenient for entries and exits, and their appearance makes them more welcoming to a child. However, the visually handicapped have difficulties in differentiating between poolside and water level in these pools, and the pool edge is difficult to grip. Also, if the pool is not properly designed it is difficult to prevent dirt from being washed back into the water.

Raised Edge Pools

These pools can be useful for those using wheelchairs who can transfer directly from the chair on to the poolside if the height is suitable. However, the raised edge can complicate entries by presenting a hurdle to be climbed over.

Poolside Design Considerations

(i)   The drop into the water should not be greater than 30cm (12in).
(ii)   Too deep a shallow end will make lifting inconvenient.
(iii)   A shallow/learner pool, with a depth of approximately 1m (3ft 3in) is required for small children.
(iv)   An adult of average height requires a depth of not less than 1.2m (3ft 11in). Many disabled people swim at an angle of 45 degrees and a shallow water pool would cause problems for them.

Catering

Warm drinks and food are much appreciated by both swimmers and spectators. There should be easy access to the areas providing a catering service. Time spent in the cafeteria often gives a very valuable opportunity to meet other people and for some people this socialisation is as important as the actual swimming experience.

Hygiene

All swimmers should develop good habits of personal cleanliness. From babies to adults the same routine should be followed. Pupils should be free of infectious diseases, open or running sores, skin infection, discharge from the ears or inflamed eyes. Before entering the pool all swimmers should visit the toilet, and take a shower. Any garments worn for swimming must be scrupulously clean and caps should be worn for both hygiene and safety. Following the swim, another quick shower should be taken. Careful drying with a clean, dry towel is important, particularly drying between the toes and drying the hair. This care is very important for babies, and swimmers who may be more delicate as a result of their disabilities.

Incontinence

Some babies and adults may be incontinent. This may deter the teacher from accepting them into swimming groups. It may in fact deter the person concerned from considering swimming as a suitable sport. An understanding of the nature of the problem and various methods of dealing with it may help.

A baby who has not gained bladder control should not go into the pool too soon after a feed and should be toileted immediately before entering the water. Towelling or other protective pants can be worn under the swimming costume. As parents accompany the babies in the water they are usually aware if there is a need for the baby to go to the toilet and can quickly leave the water. It is rare that there are accidents in parent and baby classes if this regime is followed.

Incontinence is perhaps the most difficult problem that people with disabilities such as spina bifida or paraplegia have to face. It is considered socially unacceptable and discussing it may cause embarrassment. It is caused by paralysis of the stomach and bladder muscles. Incontinence may be only of urine, but sometimes both the bladder and bowels may be affected. Some people, through mental handicap, have a lack of awareness of self-help and for them toilet training is difficult or virtually impossible.

The swimming teacher needs to be aware of the methods of managing incontinence. Swimmers requiring help should make a supervised visit to the toilet before swimming and wear a spare pair of protective pants beneath the swimming costume. Where there is no sensation but slight muscle control in the involuntary muscles of the sphincter, manual expression can be used. This will empty the bladder prior to entering the pool. The usual method is to place the hands over the front of the body just above the pubic area and to push inwards and downwards. This compresses and assists in emptying the bladder. Swimmers may perform this themselves or a child may require the help of a parent or physiotherapist.

Where a urinary diversion operation has been performed there should be complete independence. The bag, depending upon its type and its placing, may be removed for swimming and the catheter plugged, or, having been emptied it may be worn inconspicuously beneath the swimming costume.

Hygiene Aids

The following aids should be available:

(i) A plentiful supply of towels can be particularly useful for swimmers who need to dry wet wheelchairs or sit around waiting to be dried. A pile of towels may be used to cover the poolside or a bench and large, strong towels may be useful in assisted entries.

(ii) Plastic, anti-verruca socks are

sometimes worn to prevent the spread of warts. They also serve as a useful aid for paraplegics, protecting feet with impaired sensation from abrasions.

(iii)   A box of tissues is a necessity for people susceptible to respiratory infections and runny noses, and is specifically required for babies and those suffering from cystic fibrosis.

(iv)   Plastic pants or rubbers which may be worn underneath the swimming costume act as a form of extra protection against incontinence.

(v)   A fishing net can be valuable for collecting faeces after an accident. Pool purification should be adjusted after such an occurrence.

(vi)   A disinfectant footbath, trough or mat should be provided.

Safety

All swimmers should be familiar with safety regulations. Safety factors are even more important when teaching swimmers who may be more vulnerable to hazards and slower to react to warnings. Everyone teaching or helping in a swimming pool should observe the rules of safety applicable to that pool. Teaching swimming safely is dependent upon a teacher who organises well, has good discipline, is constantly aware of the whole class and avoids having pupils in a potentially dangerous situation. The teacher should be aware of the following:

(i)   Know the safety regulations and the location and use of the relevant equipment, which should be constantly checked.

(ii)   Be familiar with emergency exits and drills and devise clear emergency procedures. If an emergency arises the teacher of the class must be able to organise a quick exit from the pool. There should be adequate helpers to assist in such an emergency.

(iii)   Insist that pupils bring towels on to the poolside for use should there be an emergency.

(iv)   Have a clear visual signal for a class of hearing-impaired pupils to indicate that they must stop activity or leave the pool.

(v)   Have auditory signals for the visually impaired.

(vi)   Have an emergency drill, regularly practised with the mentally handicapped, checking that a group of slow learners has an immediate response to a blast of a whistle. Very firm discipline during these rehearsals is vital.

(vii)   Ensure that all helpers are familiar with safety procedures and are aware of the safety needs of each pupil.

(viii)   Be aware of swimmers who need to take regular medication. Activity increases the metabolism and, therefore, the passage and concentration of medication within the body. Timing the provision of the medication to occur just before swimming would ensure that the pupil is medicated throughout the session.

(ix)   Consult parents and general practitioners, and record relevant details and medication. Reports should always be kept safely, but available for ready reference if necessary during a practical session.

(x)   Check that neither swimmers nor helpers wear jewellery, and that fingernails are short.

(xi)   Use a partner or 'buddy' system to develop a caring attitude and give help when necessary in an emergency.

Whilst safety awareness must always be important for any teacher, over-anxiety must be avoided, otherwise it will be communicated to the pupil who might feel uncomfortable and over-protected.

Life-Guarding

Anyone acting as a life-guard must be aware of the special needs of swimmers. In addition to the normal skills, at any session where there are swimmers with special needs a life-guard should be conversant with certain additional skills, and also aware of particular problems that may affect a rescue attempt. Factors the life-guard should be aware of include:

(i)   Artificial respiration and cardiac compression should be known for babies, children and adults.

(ii)   The teacher must know the specific emergency drill applicable to certain swimming groups (such as visually impaired).

(iii)   Any non-contact rescue communication between the casualty and rescuer may be complicated if the casualty has sensory impairment. Appropriate visual or tactile cues may have to be used in addition to or instead of verbal communication.

(iv)   A degree of understanding of how the rescuer intends to help may not always be present so lack of co-operation may make the rescue difficult.

(v)   Contact towing rescues may be necessary more often when rescuing swimmers with disabilities.

(vi)   Landing a casualty who has very limited body movement or is very heavy may be impossible by the conventionally accepted methods. A two or three-person lift which prevents harm to the casualty should be used if possible. This can be a horizontal lift or a chair lift.

(vii)   It may be easier and safer to apply artificial respiration whilst the casualty is still in the water. There is no waste of time and it avoids what may be an uncomfortable and difficult lying position on land for people with disability.

(viii)   Life-guards should always be alerted to the presence in the water of a swimmer with a history of epilepsy and they should know the procedure to be taken.

All swimmers, including those with disability, should be taught safety, survival and life saving skills according to each individual's ability. Even those with limited physical ability can be made aware of safety factors in swimming. In particular, they need to appreciate the difference between a warm, still, supervised pool and an open water situation which may be cold, rough, murky and unsupervised. It is important even for good swimmers to be aware of their limited ability to cope with an open water situation and its invisible dangers.

2 The Principles and Methods of Teaching

Teachers of swimmers with special needs should be especially aware of individual requirements. The range of abilities of these people is extensive, not only because disabilities differ widely in type but also because the effects of any type are different for each person. The effects for each person are unique and, therefore, the teacher will find each person's needs are unique.

Because the range of ability is so extensive the teacher must develop further the basic teaching skills of observation, assessment, analysis, preparation, organisation, communication, evaluation and record keeping, as well as knowledge of skill acquisition. For example, pupils will need to be assessed in terms of mental, physical, social and emotional development and the findings related to the skills to be taught, the criteria for successful achievement and the method of teaching to be adopted. Behaviour and abilities will need to be finely analysed to identify the initial baseline and prospective achievable parts for some pupils with severe learning problems. Individual programmes with quite different emphases may need to be planned for a group with the same type and general degree of disability. Organisation will be more complex, particularly if a number of helpers are required both in and out of the water. Communication skills must be extended if working with pupils with sensory disabilities. Detailed evaluations will need to be regularly recorded to ensure continuous progress and appropriate teaching strategies to suit different aspects, stages and rates of development.

Learning

Motivation, stimulation, achievement and knowledge of results are essential in learning. Learning is an active process. Pupils should enjoy what they are doing and achieve a measure of success each lesson. Lessons should be fun, tasks must be worthwhile, the pace of the lesson varied, the teaching method appropriate and the teacher's enthusiasm and empathy evident throughout.

The initial expectations and aspirations of pupils will vary according to their previous experience, that is, the quality of the experiences they were offered and the number of their successes and failures. When planning activities the teacher must find out what each pupil can achieve to identify a baseline from which to start, then decide what may be achieved next, the stimulation for achieving it, and a method for reinforcing the correct responses and the criteria for success, or the conditions for acceptable achievement (where the activity must be done, how, and how many times). The task must be meaningful to the individual. A degree of prediction can be made by the pupil if part of a new challenge is recognisable, through previous experience. Motivation is increased when the part that can be predicted is associated with previous success.

Perceptual motor skill learning involves both mental and physical activity. The rate of teaching should be adapted to the rate of learning. If skill learning is rushed the pupil may lose confidence, become frustrated and lose motivation. Activities should be selected carefully. Low organisational activities and specific lead-up stages give pupils the opportunity to succeed, to start and finish tasks and ensure sound progression from skill to skill. The many small parts of an activity should be taught separately to simplify the activity if necessary. Success fosters the desire for more success. Pleasure can be gained from repeating the 'known' but even more from overcoming the 'unknown'.

Attention should be focused on one point at a time, followed by specific feedback related to that point. The time to do this may be before, during, or after the activity, according to the needs of the learner and the type of activity. It may be necessary to start by drawing attention to parts of the body, the action, or part of the environment to help the pupil to perceive those parts as relevant to the task, or to help recall what has been done before so that previously gained knowledge can be drawn on to assist understanding of what is required. It may be necessary to encourage prediction of a possible outcome to assist decision making about what should be done and, if performance is very slow, a reminder of intentions during the activity. After the

activity it may be useful to assist identification of what has happened and to reinforce it by referring again to a body part, to a section of the activity or to a change in the environment which can be associated with success. Some pupils may need more assistance than others to achieve the task. Recognition of success, even if only for some part of the activity, by the pupil and others is probably the strongest motivator for further learning.

The teacher can help the pupils to develop self-discipline and motivation by rewarding positive behaviour and, when appropriate, ignoring negative behaviour. A variety of methods can be used, for example, facial expression, touch, gesture, further use of a piece of equipment, repetition of a favourite activity, verbal praise, further progression through additional teaching points, certificates, badges and competition. One method may be found to be particularly effective for a pupil but its appropriateness must be constantly checked as too much repetition can have the opposite effect and lead to lack of motivation.

Beginners and the less confident need immediate feedback on their effort, relevant action they take and/or improvement they make. As they become more able and confident, the amount of attention the teacher focuses on them should be gradually reduced. They will be well on the way to developing self-discipline and motivation if they need only intermittent praise and information from the teacher to maintain the same degree of relevant effort.

A skill well learned is usually well retained. Repetition will help pupils to understand and retain movement patterns but, to maintain interest, practices should be varied, using different stimuli such as games, music and words.

The teacher should foster application of what is learned in one situation to a number of situations. The more that what is learned can be transferred, the more useful this learning becomes, in or away from the pool. Emphasising the similarity between tasks will facilitate transfer and generalisation.

Communication

The way in which a teacher communicates establishes the right atmosphere for teaching. Facial expression and body language should convey an amiable manner, patience, empathy and enthusiasm. Presentation should be multi-sensory as, generally, the greater the number of senses awakened in teaching a skill the faster and more permanent its learning.

Multi-Sensory Approach

Visual
One of the most effective ways of learning is to see the movement performed. Visual guidance is only effective if the pupils' attention is directed to a particular part of the activity, and followed immediately by the pupils trying the movement in the water, with feedback on their progress. Visual guidance may also be through charts, films and slides.

Manual
For some people this may be the most valuable means of learning, but it must always be done sensitively. It may involve the teacher in touching the arm or leg that has to be moved, guiding body parts through desired limb tracks, or a pupil feeling the desired pattern of movement performed by another swimmer.

Verbal
The language must be clearly understood, which may mean using a limited vocabulary, short simple phrases and a gradual introduction of new words. People with a hearing impairment may use other communication skills: lip-reading, signing and/or finger spelling. It could be advantageous for the teacher to follow a course in total communication to become proficient in the skills the swimmer uses. When teaching a person who lip-reads the teacher must face the pupil if possible at the same eye level and continue to speak clearly, at a normal pace, and without exaggerated movements of the mouth.

Teaching Strategies

Teaching strategies should be varied according to need. It may be necessary, at times, for the teacher to take an authoritarian role, explicitly directing the pupil through each part of the task. Another time the teacher may present the task as a problem to be solved, guiding the pupil forward through questions which may contain or convey an answer, or encourage experimentation and selection of a solution. Another strategy is for one pupil to teach another, in which case the teacher discusses intentions, strategies and progress with the pupil-teacher, not with the pupil-learner. It may be found that progress is most rapid when the teaching strategy allows the pupil to decide what he/she would like to learn and the help required from the teacher. For some, joint planning of objectives and a programme may be a very productive way of fostering learning.

Movement Exploration

This is a method of teaching where pupils are encouraged to think round problems and solve them through inventive movement. Opportunity is given to every pupil to explore, discover, select and consolidate his/her own ways of meeting the challenges set by the teacher. Tasks are set which motivate and stimulate pupils to develop an awareness of their own bodies. The teacher should present progressively demanding problems which encourage body management in water. Teacher observation of individual responses to selected tasks and careful guidance of individual pupils should result in lively and inventive movements and an improvement in confidence.

Some examples of the type of problem which can be set are:

(i) Can you touch and name different parts of your leg?
(ii) Can you make different shapes with your legs?
(iii) Can you show two ways of travelling backwards?
(iv) Can you move through a hoop with different body parts leading?
(v) Can you change from your front to your back slowly, or quickly?
(vi) Can you change level, be high then low?

Teaching those with Severe Learning Difficulties

Teachers should aim to:

● Overcome apprehension through a fun approach.
● Improve co-ordination and motor skills.
● Teach self-help skills including undressing and dressing.
● Extend communication skills.
● Reinforce academic skills and the ability to follow directions.

An environment which is conducive to learning is important. For the severely mentally handicapped this means, initially, a limited working area, removal of distractive elements, the establishment of routines, the introduction of favourite toys, songs and activities into the programme and a trusting relationship formed with a teacher or helper. Personalities differ and it is the teacher's responsibility to try to ensure a good match. A marked change in a severely handicapped pupil's behaviour and progress can occur when a mismatch is corrected. However, sustained dependence on one teacher or helper should be avoided.

Presentation of information should be multi-sensory, visual, verbal and manual. Language must be carefully planned, using simple, short sentences with a useful self-guiding word placed at the end, where it can be most easily recognised and remembered. The teacher should repeat the word for and with the pupil until the pupil can direct himself. Even if communication is difficult, it is important to convey what is about to happen and to provide knowledge of results. Posture, gesture, facial expressions and touch are all ways of conveying information. Some pupils find touch is especially important, as it conveys respect, concern and control.

The competent swimming teacher is practised in observing and identifying parts within a whole. This is especially important when teaching the mentally handicapped, for achievable steps may be very small. A skill can be broken down into many small tasks which can be learned gradually in sequence by forward and backward chaining, helping the pupil to recognise and carry out the first and last parts and gradually adding successive tasks until the whole is successfully completed. Going down the steps may involve many separate activities – looking towards, looking at, moving towards, standing by, standing between hand rails, touching and so on. To shape behaviour, any response which leads towards achieving what is desired should be rewarded. Undesired responses should be totally ignored unless there is danger to self or others, or the behaviour is so disruptive that it might interfere with the learning of others in the group.

Practice, using different approaches, is very important, but a great deal of experience may be necessary before the severely mentally handicapped person realises what is required. However, once the activity is well learned it will be retained and there may be transfer of the skill, knowledge and attitude to other activities; confidence gained through activities in water may improve self-confidence and movement performance on land.

Pupils with Temporary Severe Learning Problems

Pupils with a temporary severe learning problem may need the same or similar considerations to those shown above. For example, a previously competent adult swimmer whose body concept and self-concept has changed, due to a stroke or amputation, and who has a severe loss of self-confidence, will initially need to work one-to-one in the water for support, intensive feedback and encouragement. Preferably this should be within a supporting group who provide additional stimulation. The choice of group must always be carefully considered as it will convey a clear message of the teacher's expectation to the pupil and to others. For this type of person a written record of challenges, such as a copy of agreed task criteria and dates when achieved, could be a very useful reference for the pupil, being a proof of achievement and progress and instigation for further success.

The Pupil's Views

It is important to find out what the 'customer' thinks about his/her progress and expectations, what he/she enjoys most, dislikes, can do well, needs to practise more, would like to spend more time doing, or would like an opportunity to try. Views may also be sought about other aspects, such as the facilities, the lesson, the teaching syle, the presentation, the organisation, the amount and usefulness of the teaching or the assistance given in the changing room.

Different methods may be used to gather the information, by using informal discussion or questionnaire sheets, or by enquiring directly from the pupil or someone who will convey views for him/her. What is most important is that the pupil and the person speaking for the pupil knows that the teacher places value on what is expressed and will bear it in mind when planning programmes.

The Use of Buoyancy Aids in Teaching

The use of buoyancy aids in teaching needs a very sensitive and understanding approach if they are not to be misused. It is distressing to see a child or adult swimming with too many or incorrectly used aids. There are a number of recognised disadvantages and advan-tages in using buoyancy aids in swimming.

Disadvantages

(i) Some aids, like inflatable arm-bands and rings, can be restrictive to movement.

(ii) Inappropriate use of aids can also lead to misunderstanding of balance, i.e. arm-bands may have a stabilising effect for a pupil who feels unstable and tends to rotate around the longitudinal axis, which prevents the pupil from learning to balance himself.

(iii) Aids can be a safety risk in deep water and must be checked at regular intervals for wear and tear.

(iv) Aids can establish a feeling of false security.

Fig 1   A variety of buoyancy aids.

(v) If they are worn incorrectly, for example having too large a ring without a shoulder strap attached, they can cause an accident, or they may tilt the swimmer into an unnatural body position.

(iv) Pupils may become too dependent on one specific aid. This problem can be avoided by: regularly varying the types of aid used; making a habit of deflating the aid slightly; encouraging the pupil to get involved in fun activities which take his mind off the aids; not allowing any child to wear the aids for longer than they are needed.

Advantages

The advantages of buoyancy aids can outweigh any disadvantages and, in fact, an awareness of disadvantages and how they can be overcome can be a positive factor. To use buoyancy aids successfully, however, it is vital that each item of equipment is selected for its value for each individual pupil.

Buoyancy aids are valuable because they ensure that all pupils are safely supported and give safety in a game situation. They also give the timid pupil confidence, and give pupils opportunities for indendent movement and freedom from the beginning of the swimming programme. Buoyancy aids enable stroke practice to be tackled more easily and allow the swimmer who is not particularly able to join safely in a group fun activity.

The Use of Teaching Aids

The use of a wide selection of teaching aids stimulates pupils' curiosity and enjoyment, serving as a motivational influence conducive to further learning. Teaching aids may constitute a security prop in the form of a favourite toy, and may encourage the development of a particular skill or water adjustment. They can also serve as fun and games.

These aids may be purchased from toy shops, sports shops, equipment agents or they may originate from household, everyday items. Providing they are safe to use in water, any size, shape or texture may be used, bright colours being particularly important. For babies and the mentally handicapped, bright coloured objects in the pool may be the key to success. Teaching aids which can serve as stimuli for touch, vision and hearing should be available. Auditory aids such as music and percussion are particularly valuable in stimulating movement and interest.

The Use of Music in Teaching

Music can play a very important part in teaching those with special needs. It can be used as stimulation for movement for some people, or to encourage relaxation for others. It can be used as background music to create an atmosphere, or be used to give an accompanying rhythm for exercises or movement. The music chosen must be appropriate to the mood of the movement and the age and ability of the swimmers. For parent and baby classes, music can give a happy background sound. For adult groups, the synchronisation of swimming movements with music adds interest and encourages continuous effort in a fitness programme. A lively tune should inspire energetic movements in the water whereas slow

Fig 2   Teaching aids.

passages of music should be interpreted using slower, more gentle movements. Teachers should use music to enhance their work and to add interest, but it should be used with discretion. Constant background noise which has no meaning in the lesson inhibits both teaching and learning.

Singing

Group singing can influence the development of social relationships, can help to lessen behaviour disturbances in individuals, and can stimulate speech formation and overcome fearfulness. The most effective songs to choose are action songs. However, the choice of song should always be governed by the needs of the group; teachers should find out the musical background of the group and the programmes they enjoy. Action songs can be used especially in parent and baby classes to encourage body awareness and group movement.

Instrumental Activities

Drums, tambourines and tambours are all valuable percussion instruments which assist the achievement of rhythm, and they can be flexibly adopted to suit the working situation. A useful activity is to encourage the individual or group to synchronise movement to a clearly defined beat. Examples of activities include:

(i) Swimmers travel forwards, backwards, or sideways, to a rhythm and change direction as indicated by a heavier beat or change of rhythm.

(ii) Swimmers scull to a drum beat, head first, on the spot, then feet first, changing scull every time there is a heavier beat.

(iii) Swimmers submerge on a drum beat or, moving around, submerge on a drum beat and pick up an object upon this signal.

The Use of Games in Teaching

Games in water can be enjoyable, whilst also serving as a medium for the improvement of swimming ability. They should be carefully selected to match the needs of individuals or groups. A game used to encourage an awareness of different body parts will be applicable to babies or pupils with learning difficulties, for instance, whereas volleyball will be enjoyed by most adult groups.

Games should encourage maximum activity, so teams should be small. To encourage safe and free particpation it may be necessary for some players to use buoyancy aids, or for players to receive support or guidance from a partner or helper.

As well as being an enjoyable way of developing confidence or water stamina, games can have other uses also. They may help language use, colour recognition, the use of space, directionality, and partner and group co-operation and competition. The successful use of games often depends upon a lively and imaginative teaching approach, resulting in an exciting and stimulating swimming

Fig 3   A small group game, with two teams of three players each.

programme. Teaching through games can guarantee total involvement providing it is well planned. From the apprehensive beginner to the boisterous, confident swimmer, here is an excellent opportunity to involve the entire class together in one activity, temporarily counteracting the inevitable effects of ability group segregation. Occasionally the children or adults who are reluctant to relinquish their tight grasp on the pool rail will be motivated to join in an exciting activity, which promotes more rapid adjustment to water. In a games-like activity, many watermanship and swimming skills can be incorporated.

Very few games which are played on land cannot be adapted to the swimming pool. The teacher's sources, therefore, are limitless. Team games, relay games, tags, circle and group games and creative games can all be modified in various ways. The rules, or equipment, may be altered, and playing areas or numbers involved can be varied.

Games are most frequently developed as a contrasting activity to the lesson and played at the end, but they may be interspersed as the teacher feels appropriate, or may form the main theme of the lesson. A water games period may be a major part of an adult fitness session.

Examples of some games are given in Appendix 3 (*see* page 149), and each game can be selected or adapted to suit different ages, different physical and mental abilities, the size of pool and the size and interest of the group.

Safety

Players who are excited and involved in group activities are bound to be more at risk, so teachers must be alert.

(i)   Buoyancy aids should be worn by *any* pupils who are likely to be insecure or at risk when out of their depth.
(ii)   Deep water should be roped off if it is not to be used.
(iii)   Rules should be clear, and adhered to by all.
(iv)   Skills should be appropriate to the ability level of the swimmers.
(v)   Adequate supervision is vital and class control must be firm.
(vi)   Colours should be worn to differentiate teams, and sides should be as evenly matched as possible.
(vii)   Numbers in teams should be small to give the opportunity for maximum participation.

Lesson Planning

Each swimming lesson should be planned in advance and should be part of a scheme of work designed to provide a progressive and comprehensive swimming education. All lessons should take into consideration the facilities available and the special needs of the individuals or group, the age and ability of the swimmers and the number of helpers available. The lesson should consist of a number of purposeful activities within the capabilities of the pupils whilst still presenting an achievable challenge. Well planned lessons can make the teacher's work easier, give flow and continuity and a progressive and interesting teaching session.

Lesson Plans and Assessment Sheets

Examples of lesson plans are given in Appendix 1, and an assessment sheet in

Appendix 2. Individual teachers will select different forms of lesson plans according to their preference and the suitability of that plan for parent and baby, adult groups or for swimmers with disability. Whatever plan is used there are certain factors which should be common to each lesson:

(i)   There should be a warm-up activity to start and a warm down activity to finish.

(ii)   There should be an aim for each lesson.

(iii)   There should be a variety of activity.

(iv)   The use of any apparatus, music, or singing, should be planned ahead.

(v)   Safety factors must be considered throughout the planning.

(vi)   The organisation of swimmers' entry to the pool, the use of the pool space and how swimmers will leave the pool must be included in the planning.

(vii)   Each lesson should be evaluated, this evaluation forming the basis for future lessons.

For some pupils, a very careful assessment needs to be made prior to their involvement in swimming, and also at regular intervals thereafter. This is particularly so for people with disability. An initial assessment would include:

(i)   Transport requirements to reach and leave the swimming pool.

(ii)   Self-help ability in dressing, showering and toilet training.

(iii)   Behaviour and social skills.

(iv)   Understanding, language and communication.

(v)   Movement ability.

(vi)   Initial water confidence or attitude.

(vii)   Method of entry into the water.

(viii)   The need for helper and buoyancy aids.

(ix)   Method of leaving the water.

As swimming lessons progress, an ongoing assessment would be added to this, comprising of:

● Development of water confidence.
● Water skill development with or without help, including:
 floatation,
 sculling,
 treading water,
 rotation,
 recovery to a safe resting position,
 movement in and through water.
● Enjoyment of the lesson.
● Involvement in individual, partner and group activities.
● Reaction to music and rhythm.

Teachers will be constantly assessing progress as they are teaching, but time should be taken to record assessment, to enable a true evaluation of progress and future procedures to take place.

31

3 The Teaching of Basic Water Skills

Everyone should benefit from and enjoy a well-planned swimming pool programme. In order to achieve this goal, the teacher must first consider the individual needs of each pupil. Preparation should also involve a consideration of many other factors, including facilities, equipment, the length of the lesson, the frequency of visits to the pool, the physical, mental and social needs of the pupils and the influence of events which may have affected a person, either emotionally or physically. The important factor is that the teacher should be flexible in the design of each programme.

A teacher should endeavour to achieve certain objectives through the programme:

(i) The development of safety techniques in water.
(ii) Interaction with others through co-operative and competitive activities.
(iii) Achievement, when possible, of individual movement in water.
(iv) The promotion of fitness, suppleness, strength and stamina.
(v) The development of body awareness, co-ordination and movement skills in water.
(vi) The development of positive attitudes to swimming.
(vii) The opportunity for each individual to derive from swimming personal satisfaction, enjoyment and fun.

The range of activities can vary from an individual simply enjoying the sensation of moving in water, learning basic strokes and acquiring survival skills, to synchronised swimming or competitive swimming skills. The initial introduction to water activities, at whatever age, is of vital importance, but when teaching adults or pupils with impairments the teacher must also carefully and continuously assess the ability of all individuals and their reaction to the swimming programme.

The teacher, through an understanding of the fundamentals of how the body reacts in water and a knowledge of the basic stroke techniques, is able to plan a suitable programme for each individual. The initial goal is for everybody to swim independently using the main stroke techniques, but for many this will not be possible because of their physical or mental capacity for learning certain skills. By analysing the factors which enable us to swim the teacher will be able to establish what selection of activities and teaching methods should be used.

Buoyancy

All human bodies react in water in the same way – the heavier parts tend to sink lower than the lighter parts. Buoyancy enables the body to float, whilst 'upthrust' is the force the water applies to a body. The composition of the body, the proportion and distribution of bone, muscle and fat are the factors which determine a person's ability to float. The teacher must make certain observations, and ask, does the person:

- Float easily and very high in the water?
- Find it difficult to float?
- Float in a vertical position with low legs but with the head above the water?
- Float partially, in which there may be lack of upthrust from the water for one extremity?
- Become so tense through fear that a floating position is difficult to obtain?

Body Position and Balance

Whilst a person's natural build obviously plays a crucial role in achieving a comfortable floating position, floating is a skill which needs to be taught and adapted to the individual. A balanced float has been achieved when the body is no longer rotating in any direction and has come to rest supported by the water. Frequently, swimmers will not allow the body to continue rotating until it has reached this state of equilibrium. A desirable floating position need not be horizontal, although a clear breathing position is essential. In fact, the face may be the only part of the body which remains clear of the water.

Fig 4   Learning to achieve a prone floating position, spreading arms and legs to help balance.

An obese swimmer will float very high in the water but may find it difficult to regain a standing position. If there is fat distribution around the hips and thighs this will give buoyancy in the lower half of the body, a feeling of tipping and a sensation of fear, particularly if this physique is associated with a heavy head. The body can be made 'top heavy' when the person has no legs, and balance in water is difficult also for a swimmer without arms. A good lung capacity will aid buoyancy, and inhaling to fill the lungs with air can turn a 'sinker' into a 'floater'. For those who have poor breath control or severely reduced lung capacity floating may be difficult, depending upon the build of the body.

A stable float is achieved when the body's centre of buoyancy (centre of upward forces) is in line with the centre of gravity (centre of downward pull). For some people with heavy muscular legs, this means a vertical floating position, and for a person with more fat around the hips, a horizontal floating position.

Altering the body shape in the water can influence the position of these two centres of forces. Lifting the arms above the head moves the centre of gravity nearer to the centre of buoyancy, while curling the legs under the body moves the centre of gravity to directly under the centre of buoyancy, giving a very stable 'jelly fish' float position.

Archimedes' principle states that the more water a body displaces the more upthrust is transferred to that floating body. Therefore it is important to displace the maximum volume of water for maximum buoyancy. The head in particular needs to be submerged as much as possible whilst leaving a clear airway. With the head well back and with both

Fig 5   Stable 'jelly fish' float position; the arms circle the legs to hold a tuck position.

arms and legs in the water the body is better supported. Spasticity in one or more limbs which might cause an arm, for example, to be raised above the water, results in difficulties in floating, as that arm is not supported in the water and will increase the weight out of the water so disturbing body balance and buoyancy.

Many pupils are unhappy about extending their heads back into the water because it causes their legs to rise higher; where the legs are already buoyant there is a tendency to feel uncomfortable and out of control. These pupils will not be happy lying in such a position unless they are confident about recovery back to a resting position. It may be necessary initially to encourage the head to be held higher to help body control.

Mention has already been made of the effect of the head position or poor muscle control on balance, and particularly in the early stages consideration and understanding is needed by the teacher. The head is often vital in instigating a change in body position, and it initiates rotation around the body's horizontal and vertical axes. If it sinks into the water, it may cause a feeling of loss of control and may result in panic. A pupil may need to hold the head high and to have adequate practice of rotation and recovery skills. Learning to rotate or balance is an important part of learning to float for those people whose body is more asymmetrical or one-sided. Even when action is severely restricted, a pupil may learn to counteract rotation by turning

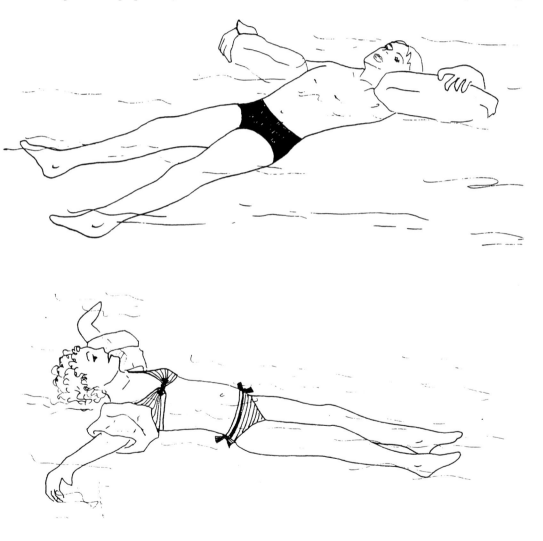

Fig 6   Buoyancy aids used to help balance when learning a supine float.

the head in the opposite direction. Arm and leg movements can also be used to aid balance. An individual should experiment by crossing the legs or stretching them wide, and extending an arm or reaching across the body. Anyone who experiences balance problems will need to experiment with the above movements until they have established a means of counteracting rotation in the water.

People who suffer from the effects of poor muscle control and uncontrolled, unpredictable limb movements may also experience great difficulties when learning to float. A head support may be needed to prevent the head extending suddenly backwards and underwater. A teacher should encourage the pupil to relax, to allow the pressure of the water to slow down uncoordinated movements. Some people may find it acceptable to rely on buoyancy aids, but every pupil should have some time totally unaided and should be given the opportunity to experience the sensation of buoyancy. Buoyancy aids can create a stabilising effect, and may eliminate balance problems, but they should be used only as a stage towards learning unaided floatation and balance.

Having assessed the swimmer's ability to float it is necessary to assess the limb movement. In swimming, propulsion is gained from the arms and legs acting as levers, and from the hands and feet acting as paddles. For swimmers with limited mobility in the shoulders and hips, movement through the water is still possible if good sculling actions are taught, maximising the available movement to give a propeller-type action and using any flexibility of the hands and feet.

The teacher should assess the pupil's range of movement in the joints and the power which the limb can generate. The co-ordination of movements is also important for, though isolated limb movements may be performed satisfactorily, the skill may break down when combined with movements of the other limbs.

The teacher can test the range of movement by asking the swimmer to move each limb joint by joint. If it is feasible, observe these movements when the swimmer is in the water and as relaxed as possible, perhaps using artificial aids or a partner to help balance. However, the aids must not inhibit the range of movement. As the arms give the greatest propulsion in most strokes, begin by assessing the movement potential in the upper limb girdle.

To assess the shoulder joint, the pupil must be asked whether the arm can be stretched above the head. The teacher should note how close the upper arm is to the ear, as this will indicate the suitable entry point for an arm stroke. It should then be assessed how far behind and in front of the body the arm can be taken, as this will indicate whether out of water arm recoveries require adaptation. The pupil should be asked to take the arm out to the side and across the body. Are these shoulder joint movements performed easily and with relaxation or are they forced and involving associated movements of the trunk?

In assessing the elbow joint the teacher should establish whether there is a full range of flexion and extension. This should be tested out of the water and then under the water to assess if the movement is possible against water resistance. Maximum propulsion is achieved from a bent elbow action, but a slower yet satisfactory swimming stroke may use little flexion in the elbow. The teacher must also establish how much flexion and extension there is in the wrist joint, how much sideways flexion abduction and adduction there is and whether the swimmer can fully extend the fingers.

A good way to test the effectiveness of the hand is to ask the swimmer to stand or kneel with shoulders submerged and to try a sculling action just a few inches below the surface of the water. This continuous action with the little finger uppermost on the outward swirl, then the thumb uppermost on the inward swirl, gives a changing pitch of the hand. This action produces a vortex close to the water surface. The stronger the action, the bigger the vortex. The ability to change the pitch of the hand will create lift or thrust during arm movements in swimming. The smallest vortex shows that propulsion from sculling is to be anticipated.

This observation of the upper limb girdle flexibility, strength and relaxation should indicate to the teacher how to achieve the optimum use of the arms in swimming.

The lower limb girdle should be observed in a similar way. Some swimmers can achieve a greater range of movement in the hip when the body is supported by the water and may even be able to 'walk' in the water, whilst not being able to do so on land. In assessing the hip joint one should ask whether the legs can be moved forwards, backwards, sideways and in what range; is there rotation in the hip joint? It should be noted whether the knee joint can be bent and stretched when under the water and, to assess the ankle joint, whether the foot can trace a circle. Can the foot be stretched (plantar flexed) and bent (dorsi flexed)?

The teacher should observe how movement in one joint may affect that in another joint of the same limb. For instance, there may be a composite hip, knee and ankle flexion. This assessment of the movement in the lower limb will determine how far the legs can be used to help balance the body and if they can add to the propulsive power of the stroke. For some they may offer the main source of propulsion, and suitable stroke patterns to maximise this should be selected.

Having assessed the ability of the limbs in isolation the co-ordination of the movements of the limbs should be observed. This is done through looking at simple symmetrical and asymmetrical paddling actions, first of the arms using a simple back or front paddle, then of the legs, then combined. Are symmetrical or asymmetrical actions easier? Which is the most effective? How successful are movements requiring arm and leg co-ordination? Do arm and leg movements cause a marked change in the balance of the body in the water? By asking for a change in the tempo of an action, slow to fast for instance, the teacher can observe whether there is any change in muscle tension or involvement of other parts of the body.

This assessment will be carried out whilst a swimmer is being introduced to the water through a watermanship programme. For all non-swimmers certain water orientation skills should be learnt before progressing to the basic swimming strokes.

A Watermanship Programme

This programme should aim to give balance and confidence in the water. It should not be rushed and should incorporate fun activities which help to establish skills. The pupils should be fully involved in the learning situation. They should know why they are asked to move in a particular way or why they carry out a selected practice. The teacher should ask questions also, in order to draw information from the pupils, a procedure which will encourage full involvement as well as operate as a check of their understanding up to that point. The pupil will gain confidence in the teacher through the presentation of carefully graded tasks, with time given for repetition. Acute teacher observation can help the pupils' attention and interest, since a positive relationship develops through constant teacher/pupil communication, and performance can be constantly refined and reinforced. Skill development should be an individualised procedure, with pupils being challenged by their own needs. This can be best achieved by the teacher adopting a flexible teaching approach and setting tasks which pupils can answer at their own level and in their own way.

The lesson's content must be carefully selected to provide enjoyable activities which are fun to perform and which give a sense of achievement, success and challenge. Material must be selected to suit the physical and mental ability and the age of the pupils. Buoyancy aids should be used to encourage freedom of movement and to help balance in these early stages. Whenever possible, when a skill has been performed and practised

using aids it should then be practised with reduced use of or no buoyancy aid. Some pupils, particularly those with severe physical or mental impairment, will require help from a competent partner.

With all non-swimmers it is important to establish certain skills:

- Methods of entry into the pool.
- A variety of floating positions.
- Regaining a standing position or recovery to a safe breathing and resting position.
- Maintenance of regular breathing patterns.
- The ability to submerge and recover.
- A variety of ways of moving in water.
- Changing direction with ease.
- Rotating movements.
- Leaving the pool with minimal assistance.

Entries into the Pool

Some swimmers will require assistance to enter the water, the methods being explained in Chapter 4. Entry can be made by using steps in a safe manner, usually going down backwards. Alternatively, a pupil can sit on the edge with the feet in the water, twisting and stretching both arms to one side of the body to press both hands firmly on the poolside. The weight of the body is taken on the hands and the body is turned and lowered under control into the water facing the poolside, the hands still holding the edge for security.

The corner of the pool can be used to enter the water also, or a person can sit on the side and topple or roll into the water. Stepping in from a standing position, initially with help from a

Fig 8 Sitting between floats ready to move the legs in different directions.

Fig 7 Entering safely by going backwards down a vertical ladder.

partner, is another method of entry, as is jumping from the side into shoulder-depth water. A swimmer can also tip into deep water from a variety of starting positions.

Body Position, Balance, Recovery and Rotation

Water Activities

(i) With a float in each hand and with partner support if needed, 'sit up in the water', moving your legs slowly into different shapes and directions, then recover to a sitting or standing position. The teacher should encourage variety in the use of space and in the use of the head to help balance and initiate change of direction.

(ii) Float in a variety of shapes, wide, thin and round and hold the achieved shape.

(iii) Change between prone and supine floating positions, using pendulum-type or rotating movements.

(iv) Push and glide in a variety of body positions; a partner may be used to initiate movement where a push is not possible. Discover which position allows your body to travel through the water most easily in both prone and supine positions.

(v) Recover to a safe resting position from a prone horizontal position. This may be a standing position holding the rail, using the rail to achieve the vertical position or by rotating to a supine float.

(vi) Recover to a safe resting position from a supine position.

(vii) Link balance movements together, practise gliding, floating, rotating and recovering.

Fig 9   Taking the legs backwards to a horizontal position with
support from floats.

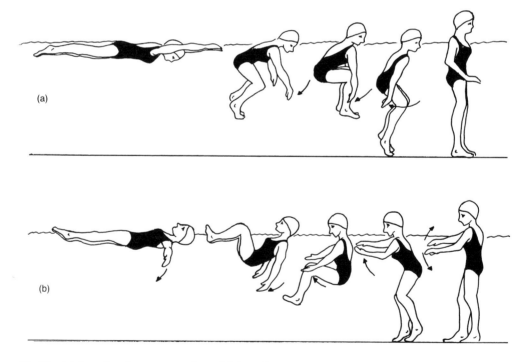

Fig 10   (a) Standing from a prone float. (b) Standing from a supine
float.

When teaching balance activities, establish a calm atmosphere by speaking quietly but clearly. To take up a floating or gliding position the swimmer should always start with the shoulders under the water, lean slowly into the position by stretching the arms out sideways to give balance, and move the head towards the direction of the float. A partner can support under the hands for a prone float or with arms held lightly under the back for a supine float. The swimmer's head can rest on the submerged shoulder of the helper.

When teaching how to regain a standing position, the teacher should emphasise the return to a *sitting* position before putting the feet down. Adults will often try to stand up by dropping the feet to the pool floor, when they might well tip, being off balance.

Give clear instruction of the stages of recovery. From prone float, the swimmer should lift the head up and press down with the hands, then tuck the knees up to the chest and finally place the feet firmly on the bottom of the pool. From supine float, the swimmer should bring the head forward, scoop the arms forward, then tuck the knees up to the chest and finally place the feet firmly on the bottom of the pool. The skill of recovery, or an alternative method of assuming a safe position, should be repeated until it is easily accomplished.

Submerging and Breath Control

If swimmers are to be able to survive independently in water, it will be necessary for them to learn to maintain a rhythmic breathing pattern whilst moving through the water. This should be encouraged from the first introduction to water, or even at home in the bath or at the washbasin, when blowing bubbles can be taught. Regular breathing is necessary if an activity is to be maintained for any length of time, and it also assists relaxation in the water. The teacher should always encourage an exhalation 'blow out' as the mouth goes near the water, inhalation following automatically.

Submerging is feared by most non-swimmers and even by some quite competent swimmers. The swimmer needs to be encouraged, but not forced, to go under the water. The teacher must be sympathetic and try to achieve results through fun activities.

Water Activities

(i)   Put your mouth on the water and blow bubbles, lifting the head to breathe in.

(ii)   Blow a table tennis ball or 'poached egg' (plastic circular toy that flips over when blown) along the surface of the water.

(iii)   Blow into the water when moving with your shoulders below the surface, holding a float in the hands. For children, the teacher could suggest they are driving a boat, the bubble sound being the engine.

(iv)   Move to music; when the music stops blow bubbles with your mouth under water.

(v)   Lower your upright body in the water until mouth and nose are under water. This can be performed holding the rail, with partner support or in a free space.

(vi)   Lower your body until the head is under the water.

(vii)   Submerge completely and hold your breath.

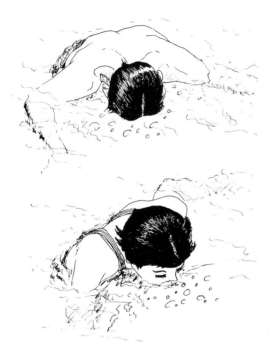

Fig 11 In a standing position, putting the face in the water to blow bubbles, lifting the head to breathe in.

(viii) Submerge and explode your breath out.

(ix) Bob up and down, exhaling under water and taking in a breath of air between each submersion.

(x) Hold hands with a partner and create a see-saw.

(xi) Move under floats, hoops, or toys placed on the water surface.

(xii) Touch the bottom of the pool with different parts of the body. The teacher should encourage eyes to be kept open under the water.

(xiii) Pick up different objects from the pool floor.

(xiv) Move to music; when the music stops pick up an object from the pool floor.

(xv) Move through submerged or semi-submerged hoops, one for each swimmer.

(xvi) Lift a ball high above the water then push it under the water, perhaps going down with it.

(xvii) With a partner, exchange a ball overhead and then between legs.

(xviii) Try a jack-in-the-box, coming up to the surface with different body parts leading.

(xix) Stand and topple into the water in different directions, to which jumping can be added if possible.

(xx) Roll in the water with the body rounded, or straight, or any other somersault and rolling type actions.

(xxi) Link movements together continuously, such as floating, rolling and recovering, submerging, lifting a limb high and recovering it, then moving under or through a hoop or a series of hoops in different ways.

Developing Movement in the Water

Moving in the water can be a very relaxing and enjoyable experience, particularly for people unable to move freely on land. For those who are severly disabled, movement may be dependent upon a partner who supports and guides them, or provides turbulence beneath a balanced gliding position and so creates movement. Whenever possible, the teacher should encourage free movement through the use of suitable buoyancy aids, and then as a knowledge of how to move is established and practised the aids can be removed.

Free movement should be encouraged through fun activities. At this stage it is enjoyment and confidence that are important rather than specific stroke techniques.

Water Activities

(i)   Push a ball along, using different parts of your body.

(ii)   With shoulders under the water, move forwards, backwards, sideways, or turn around.

(iii)   Move in different ways according to the directions given by the teacher.

(iv)   Make a 'circular' or 'square' shape while travelling through the water.

(v)   Draw a pattern with your nose or hand on the water.

(vi)   Move around hoops, going under, through, or round them.

(vii)   Move in the water by walking, jumping, skipping and taking big strides.

(viii)   Move to match the rhythm of music or percussion instruments.

(ix)   Move to collect floating objects (different coloured objects are retrieved and one at a time placed in a hoop).

(x)   Discover how the hands are used to pull or push yourself through the water.

(xi)   Push a ball or float along with feet off the pool bottom.

(xii)   Follow a partner, who changes direction or changes methods of travelling.

(xiii)   Make up a sequence of movement such as travelling forwards, backwards, turning and recovering, or travelling under the water, floating, rotating and recovering.

These movement activities, combined with floating, gliding and submerging practices, should establish a basic water confidence. Once floating and gliding has been learnt successfully a variety of sculling actions should be introduced.

Sculling

Sculling is a most important skill to develop. It is an arm and hand action used to balance, propel and control the body. Once a good sculling action is established, a swimmer can travel and turn in the water or use the action to balance horizontally or vertically. It can be a very strong and powerful action and even for swimmers with little movement or strength in their arms it can still be performed effectively. Each step towards learning to scull can be taken using buoyancy aids if required.

One basic sculling action is varied to achieve movement in different directions or to give support; this involves the arms moving away from and then towards the centre line of the body. On the outward sweep the palm is angled to face outward, little finger uppermost to lead the action. On the inward sweep the thumb leads and the palm faces inwards. The sculling action should be smooth and continuous, but the speed can be varied. This action may be described as a figure of eight movement in the water. The actual position of the arms will vary according to the buoyancy of the swimmer and the shape of the body. Normally the arms should be kept close to the body with a fairly small sideways range of movement.

Teaching Sculling

The swimmer should initially be encouraged to experiment with sculling-type actions to find out how the hands and arms move the body in different ways. If possible, have a good swimmer demonstrate sculling, particularly highlighting the position and action of the hand. Standing in shallow water with the shoulders submerged, or balancing in a vertical position helped by buoyancy aids the pupil should stretch the arms out forward along the water surface, making the sculling action following the teacher's demonstration. They should be told to feel as though they are making holes in sand with each hand. The arms remain below the water surface.

By tipping the head back from standing with shoulders submerged the swimmer can lie back and continue to scull. The arms come close to the side of the body. By turning the fingers up (wrists hyper-extended) and keeping the hands firm and flat the figure of eight movement should propel the body with the head leading. In this scull the pressure of the scull is towards the feet.

The pitch of the hand can be changed to use sculling to travel in a supine position with the feet leading (wrists flexed, fingertips to the bottom of the pool), or to travel in a prone position with the head leading (hands close to the hips, wrists flexed). Sculling can also be used to turn in the water in a tucked shape.

Water Activities
(i)   Scull to music making patterns in the pool.
(ii)   Scull to music making a sequence of different changes in direction.
(iii)   Scull with a partner, matching the pattern of your partner's movement.
(iv)   Scull with a small group making different patterns, using different sculls to fit to a phrase of music.
(v)   Scull to hold the body horizontal or vertical.

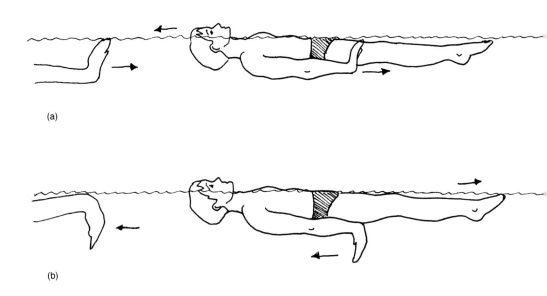

(a)

(b)

Fig 12   (a) Sculling, head leading, wrists extended. (b) Sculling, feet leading, wrists flexed.

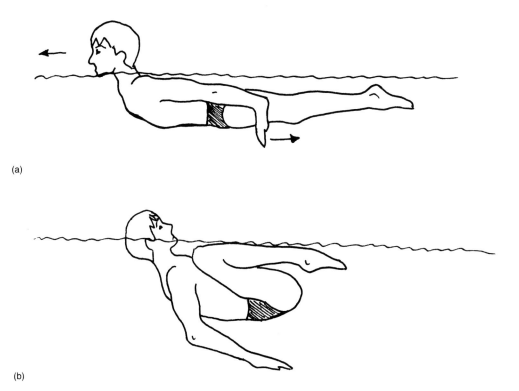

Fig 13 (a) Sculling in a prone position, wrists extended. (b) Sculling to turn in a tucked position.

Treading Water

Treading water is a basic safety skill for swimmers starting to swim unaided in deeper water. It gives a resting and safe breathing position for many swimmers and is a position in which to conserve energy. It is a means of stopping to avoid a collision, or to listen to an instruction.

Once sculling and a basic leg action have been taught, treading water can usually be achieved relatively easily. The swimmer is in a vertical position submerged up to the chin. The legs use a circular breast-stroke type action, a scissor kick or alternating flipper type action. The arms and hands use a sculling action in front of the body just under the water surface. The head should be held up, with the mouth just clear of the water to facilitate rhythmical breathing.

Teaching Treading Water

In the shallow end, teach the pupil to establish the sculling arm action. With the arms supported by two floats teach an appropriate leg action. The breast-stroke type action is most efficient, if it is possible. Treading water is a useful practice for breast-stroke leg action which often proves difficult to learn.

When the leg action is established, the pupil should release the floats and add the arm action. The pupil should now change from travelling to treading water, and attempt to turn round whilst treading water. The next step is to increase the length of time the movement can be sustained, and ideally to eliminate the use of one limb. For some swimmers with certain disabilities the skill may originally have been accomplished using only two or three limbs.

Achievements of the Programme

Such a watermanship programme, applicable to any swimmer, should develop the following: mental adjustment to the water; body buoyancy; body alignment in the water; lateral, vertical and combined rotations; balance of the body in the water in stillness and in movement; basic limb movements to aid balance and propulsion; an understanding of how and why the body balances and moves in water; and co-ordination of movements.

This level of competence gives a framework for the development of the traditional strokes. The teacher must aim to challenge all swimmers and to expect high standards of performance from them. The adaptation of swimming techniques to suit the needs of swimmers with disability requires an understanding of the fundamental principles of swimming and movement in the water. The key to success is to work towards an accepted efficient swimming stroke. Too great a divergence from this may at a later stage hamper the swimmer's progress, particularly involvement in competition.

When teaching swimmers with special needs, the stages of learning may have to be adapted. The rate of learning will of course be variable, some swimmers possibly taking years to reach a level of proficiency. The individual's performance will be affected by the impairment. Factors which affect performance include: density of the body; control of the head; buoyancy of specific body parts; absence of limbs; control of the body; breath control; muscle power; mobility in the joints; and variable attention span.

Teaching Strokes

The factors governing an efficient stroke are minimal resistance and maximum propulsion, and these should be the swimmer's aim.

Body Position

It is important that the position of the body in the water should be as streamlined as possible, bearing in mind that in some instances, it is not natural or comfortable for this to be achieved. Particularly in the early stages, some pupils are not happy with their heads back in the water as body control, recovery and balance are then impeded.

Some paraplegics find that whilst supine their legs float very high, yet whilst prone their hips float high but their legs tend to drift lower in the water. Hemiplegics may prefer to swim on the side or move vertically. If breath control is a problem, swimming on the front can be difficult; a pupil may choose to swim on the back, for example, but roll on to the front to recover to a standing position. A bobbing head action in a stroke like breast-stroke is sometimes accompanied by a steeply inclined body position. As the confidence of the swimmer grows and as that person swims faster the body position will flatten and streamlining will be improved.

Leg Actions

For many people a leg kick is not possible, and for others adaptations have to be made. When a swimmer is likely to experience difficulties with balance, particularly as a result of having no arms or being unable to move the arms, a symmetrical leg kick particularly whilst supine will create less of a rolling action. That person might prefer initially to be supine as the lack of arm movement would make a lifting movement of the head for breathing difficult. A person with stiff and painful joints will only be capable of a gentle hip and knee movement, although it is important to maintain a certain range of movement at all times.

Possible adaptations of conventional leg movements are numerous and can range from a gentle cycling leg action on the front to a dolphin leg kick initiating a body wave and porpoising movement through the water. Some people may depend entirely on a leg kick for propulsion and when the smallest degree of leg movement can be achieved it should be encouraged.

Arm Actions

The arm action in conventional strokes is usually the main source of propulsion, so if there is severe physical impairment the arm movement may need to be modified; a good sculling movement can be a great asset in this situation.

Symmetrical movements are often the easiest to co-ordinate and a breast-stroke arm action is frequently adapted to provide support as well as propulsion. A pull using more downward pressure is often best and, although not so proficient technically, is a useful adaptation.

Balance can be difficult if there is little or no leg kick, so lifting an arm for an out of water recovery in front or back crawl may cause sinking and rotation, and therefore an underwater arm recovery may prove more successful. Balance is often aided by a sculling-type movement before recovering the arm over the water to balance the body's own lateral swing. A swimmer with a paralysed arm may, when swimming on the front, pull the affected arm forward with the good arm, and then the arm would naturally flex back towards the body. This is a fairly difficult movement to achieve effectively, but some swimmers find it possible.

Breathing

Breathing should interfere as little as possible with the stroke rhythm and a rhythmical breathing pattern should be developed. The timing and type of breathing should be developed to fit the needs of the pupil and the chosen stroke.

Rhythm

A good stroke rhythm should come about through the practice of an efficient technique. The difficulty for a physically handicapped swimmer is likely to arise where there is no leg kick to balance an arm action or where the pupil is uneven or severely restricted in movement.

Pupils with obvious co-ordination problems due to lack of muscle control caused by brain damage find it extremely difficult to master the co-ordination of arms and legs. In this case, a considerably longer period of time needs to be devoted to working on legs or arms only. The combination of the two can prove exceptionally difficult to master.

Information and detailed teaching methods for the conventional strokes are available in numerous swimming books. There are, however, certain strokes using mainly underwater limb movements which give particularly useful methods of propulsion for recreational swimmers.

Side Stroke

Side stroke is an excellent stroke for recreational swimming, as the face and mouth can more easily be kept clear of the water so breathing is easier. It is also a stroke that may have been learned early by many adults now returning to swimming. It uses a scissor kick which is more natural and effective for some people, as the extent of the leg action can be adapted to the mobility and strength of the legs. The side stroke may be swum conventionally using two arms or using only the arm on the side to which the face is turned. It can be swum in an easy and relaxed manner with low energy demands being made of the swimmer.

Body Position

The side on which the swimmer lies is according to individual preference, but swimming on alternate sides should be encouraged where possible, because it is restful to change sides and it gives equal exercise to the whole body. In the glide position the body is stretched along the surface with the left or right side of the

head in the water, the chin toward the upper shoulder and the eyes looking toward the feet. The lower arm is extended straight out in front, continuing the line of the body. The top arm rests along the side of the body. The legs are extended and together, with the ankles stretched.

Leg Action

The scissor kick is the most effective leg action to use for this stroke. From the legs extended position the knees are flexed, bringing the heels towards the hips. The legs are separated and roughly parallel to the water surface, the top leg going forwards and the lower leg backwards. The legs are extended and powerfully brought together in an action similar to closing a pair of scissors, from which its name derives. As in all strokes propulsion is gained from the feet, the sole of the upper foot as it changes from a bent to an extended position pushing against the water and the front of the extended rear foot, and also by the pressing action on the water by the legs. Side stroke can be swum using adapted breast-stroke or front crawl type leg actions although they are not normally as effective.

Arm Action

From the stretch position the lower arm starts its propulsive action. The hand takes hold of the water in the catch position just beneath the surface. Power is gained from a pull/push action allied to a sculling hand action, with a thumbs-up position as the arm presses in towards the chest. The elbow is flexed but remains high, and propulsion is gained from the palm of the hand and the forearm sweep-

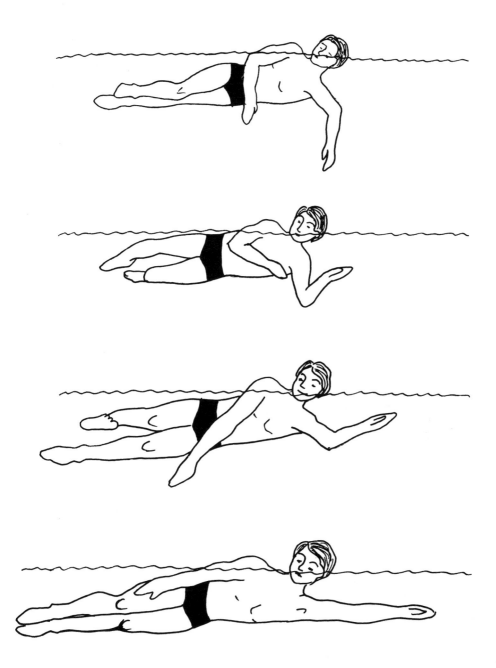

Fig 14   Side stroke; side of the head in the water, scissor leg kick,
lower arm pull-push action then upper arm pushes as it extends.

ing against the water. As the lower arm is in the propulsive phase the upper arm recovers to near the chin by bending the elbow. This arm then exerts force, the palm is turned to face backward and the palm and forearm press against the water as the arm is extended close to the body, finishing at the thigh. The lower arm recovers simultaneously to the extended gliding position. As one arm gives propulsion the other is recovering and a glide can be held between the action of the arms.

Breathing

Breathing does not cause problems in the side stroke, but it should be regular, normally with exhalation on the glide and inhalation at the end of the push phase of the lower arm.

Co-Ordination

1 From the glide; lower arm pull/push phase, upper arm and legs recovery movements, breath in.
2 Push action with upper arm, leg kick.
3 Glide action with upper arm, leg kick.
4 Glide and breathe out.
5 Pull and kick and glide helps co-ordination.

Teaching Side Stroke

(i) Establish a push and glide on the side with one arm extended forward, one by the side. Check the head position.
(ii) Isolate the leg action if necessary. This can be taught with the legs close to the pool wall, the body in a vertical position and one side of the body close to the wall to permit the forward and backward scissor action of the legs.

(iii) A float can be held by the swimmer's extended arm to allow concentration on the leg action and particularly on the use of the feet.
(iv) The arm action may be introduced by the swimmer standing in water of chest depth, bending sideways and following the action of the teacher.
(v) Co-ordinate the stroke using key words such as pull-and-push-glide or pull-push-kick-glide. Spacing of the key words when teaching emphasises the desired rhythm.

Swimming on the Back

For many people, swimming on the back gives an easy means of swimming, as the mouth is clear of the water to breathe. A variety of means of propulsion can be used, building on pushing, gliding and sculling. Having the confidence to scull in a variety of ways as already described gives a good basis for the addition of different leg actions.

The flutter kick is one leg action which can be used. Push and glide, scull with the hands, use a fast alternate leg action with power on the up kick.

An alternative is the double flutter (dolphin action) kick. The feet are held close together with the legs moved simultaneously, from the hips, up and down in the water. The arms scull, or simultaneously bend, to bring the hands close to the shoulders and then take a strong push down towards the feet, the palms of the hand leading. The arm action can be developed using an overwater double arm recovery and a strong pull/push action from above the head to the thighs.

Fig 15   Inverted breast-stroke leg action, body inclined, knees under the water, drive coming from lower legs and feet.

Inverted Breast-Stroke Leg Action

This stroke gives good propulsion without using any arm action, but can be further developed using a variety of arm actions.

Body Position

The body position is inclined slightly, with the head raised, to allow the hips to sink in the water, which is necessary to permit the underwater leg action.

Leg Action

From the back glide position the thighs are kept parallel with the surface of the water, the knees are opened slightly sideways and the feet lowered until they are below the knees with the feet turned out. The inside of the lower legs and feet drive out and round against the water to give propulsion, ending with the knees and feet close together.

Arm Action

The arm actions involved are a sculling action, and a larger sweeping action in which the hand and forearm push from the shoulders down the side of the body. A full double-arm action may also be used.

The stroke starts in a back glide position, with the arms extended above the head, the palms facing upwards just beneath the water surface. From the glide the arms take a pull/push action (double back crawl propulsive phase), ending at the thighs. The recovery may be over the water or returning to the glide position by drawing the arms under the water. The co-ordination is arms-legs-glide. The legs kick as the arms recover and they remain in the streamline position as the arms take their propulsive phase. This can be a very relaxed and leisurely stroke but can be developed to be quite powerful. Breathing should be regular and fitted in at the same phase of each stroke, exhalation occurring towards the end of the arm propulsion, and inhalation taking place during the arm recovery.

Dog Paddle

The dog paddle is a valuable stage in the learning of front crawl but it also gives an easy means of travelling on the front

51

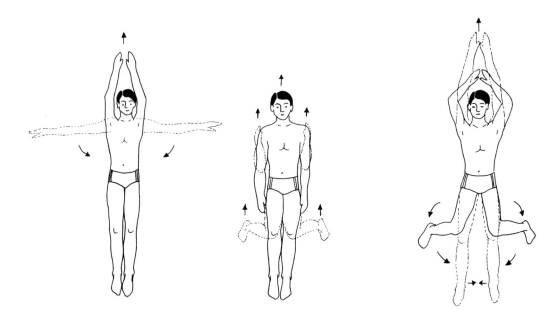

Fig 16   Backstroke; legs kick as arms recover overhead, arms pull
and push as legs are together and streamlined.

Fig 17   Dog paddle; arms remain under the water for pull and push
phase and recovery.

where an out of the water arm recovery is not possible. It can be swum with the head out of the water for easy breathing, or with the head partly in the water using either forward or sideways breathing.

Sometimes the arm action takes place in front of the shoulder line, but in extended dog paddle the arms should perform a full underwater pull/push action as in front crawl, pushing right through to the thighs. The arm is recovered under water, with an action similar to that in breast-stroke.

The leg action is normally a front crawl leg kick, but the stroke may be swum without a leg action or with a dolphin-type action.

Award Schemes

Awards can present a challenge, and used with discretion can fit into a good swimming curriculum by logical progression. Whatever their age or ability swimmers like to feel they have worked to achieve a standard, and gaining an award is a reward for effort and a motivation to achieve further skills. The ASA award scheme is wide ranging and can by careful selection offer an achievement goal for all swimmers.

Competition

Competition should be used by teachers throughout the learning of swimming. Used correctly it can be stimulating and, like awards, offers the swimmer a challenge. Competition may be against oneself or against others. There will be some swimmers who wish to participate in recognised competitive events; competitions are normally held under the auspices of an organising body and they demand adherence to a particular system of classification and rules. Teachers should contact the appropriate organisation or club to gain information on the classification systems to be used. However, independently-run local events will use a system most appropriate to the needs of the competitors and the nature of the competition. In school or club competition the aim should be for maximum involvement and enjoyment.

4 The Techniques of Lifting and Handling

Lifting and handling is a particularly practical subject and it should be noted that all the methods outlined below should be practised on an able-bodied volunteer until they can be carried out competently. Swimmers with disabilities should not be handled any more than is absolutely necessary. They should be encouraged to move by themselves whenever possible, provided that every care is taken to avoid accidents and that help is available when requested. Many people with disability are inventive and agile and will devise their own methods of transferring themselves to the poolside. Some of the lifts and supports may require modification to suit individual needs and circumstances.

Lifting may be necessary in the following instances:

- Taking a wheelchair up and down steps.
- Undressing and dressing.
- Transferring from wheelchair to poolside.
- Transferring from poolside to wheelchair.
- Toileting or showering.

Clothing

Clothes should be worn which will allow unrestricted movement, such as tracksuits; flat, well-fitting non-slip shoes should be worn, to provide a stable base; no jewellery or wrist watches should be worn.

Procedure

For any lift, a leader should always be appointed – preferably the person taking the heaviest weight. Everyone, including the person being lifted, should know exactly which lifting procedure is to be adopted.

Lifting Posture

Stand with your feet approximately hip width apart to give maximum stability. Keep close to the swimmer as this gives more control during the lift. Keep your back straight throughout the lift to prevent back injuries, and bend at the hips and knees. Tighten your abdominal muscles to avoid strain, and use strong leg and hip muscles to straighten and lift. Turn by pivoting on the heels, one at a time, and avoid twisting the back or knees as this can also lead to strain. Try to avoid carrying a patient over great distances, and be particularly aware of changes in floor level or wet, slippery surfaces.

Wheelchairs

It is advisable to use a wheelchair or shower chair for anyone who is unsteady or who normally wears callipers, special boots, or artificial limbs because they will be unsteady without their usual supports, and they may slip on the wet floor, particularly when leaning on walking sticks or other supports. After a swim, they will be tired and more likely to fall or slip. Dragging their bare feet on rough non-slip surfaces is to be avoided as it can cause abrasions.

Wheelchairs normally have brakes operated by levers, with forward and backward movements, which are usually located in front of the large wheels. Attendant-push wheelchairs usually have a pram-type brake at the back. Arm rests are usually detachable by pulling them upwards, although sometimes a lever underneath the front must be released first. Always ensure that the swimmer's arms are clear. Foot rests are plates that lift up, swing to the side, or can be detached. Users should never stand on the foot plates as this will tip the wheelchair forwards. Some chairs have a leg-divider which may need to be removed.

When using a wheelchair:

(i)   Never tip a wheelchair forward.
(ii)   Position the wheelchair sideways to the poolside in case the swimmer tips forward.
(iii)   If the brakes are not functioning adequately, the wheelchair must be placed with its back against a wall to prevent it running away. This technique may also be applied when using a shower chair which may well not have brakes.
(iv)   Remove the arm rest on the appropriate side before lifting.

(v)   Turn aside or remove the footplates to allow the helpers more space in which to work safely.

Wheelchair Lifts

Wheelchairs can be manoeuvred up or down a few steps as long as the helper can control the weight of the wheelchair and the user. *Great care* must be taken not to throw the person forward and out of the wheelchair as it is returned to the horizontal. A flight of steps should be avoided as it is *not* practical in a wheelchair.

When going up a few steps warn the swimmer what you are about to do, turn the wheelchair to take it up backwards and push down on the tipping lever with your foot. Steady the chair with the handles and carefully tip it back until it is well balanced on the back wheels. Pull the chair up the steps on the back wheels, then lower it to the horizontal, placing the front castor wheels on the ground. If needed, have a helper in front of the wheelchair who will assist by lifting the undercarriage (*not* by the footplates or arm rests).

When going down a few steps, warn the swimmer what is about to happen, face the wheelchair forward and push down on the tipping lever with your foot. Steady the chair with the handles and tip the wheelchair on to the back wheels. Edge slowly over the steps, keeping the wheelchair on its back wheels until the last step is reached. Lower the wheelchair slowly back to the horizontal.

Handling for Undressing and Dressing

Privacy should be maintained wherever possible, and help should be given discreetly and only when it is required or requested.

Lying

Children and adults who are unable to support themselves or who have poor balance (for example those with muscular dystrophy) may have to be changed whilst lying down. A large padded bench or table at wheelchair height is very convenient and to remove clothing the person can be rolled from one side to the other by pressure on the shoulders and hip.

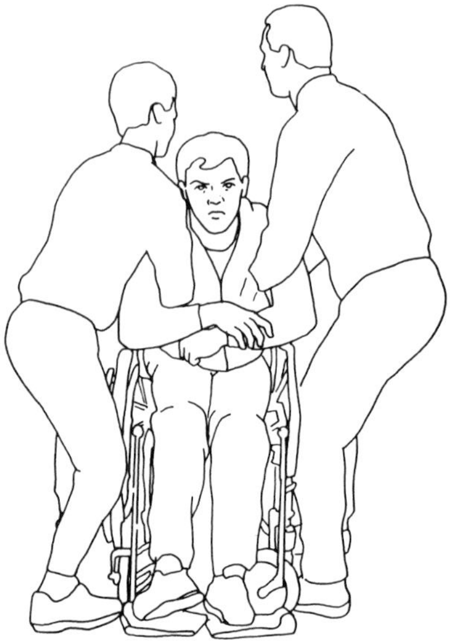

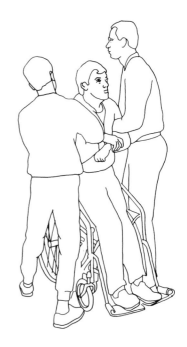

Fig 18   Through-arm lift; initial position.

In a Wheelchair

Many disabled people can undress whilst sitting in a wheelchair. Trousers, pants or tights can be removed from one side while the person leans or twists to the opposite side, so taking all the weight on one buttock.

Using a Through-Arm Lift

This lift is useful when undressing people in a wheelchair. The helpers stand close to and on each side of the wheelchair, facing the back of the chair, and hook their inside arm through the swimmer's arm, the other hand resting on the swimmer's lower back (Fig 18). The helpers should stand with feet apart and hips and knees bent. On command, the helpers straighten their legs to lift up and extend the swimmer's hips (Fig 19). The helper's rear hand can then be freed and

Fig 19   Through-arm lift; lifting to assist dressing.

used to assist with undressing the swimmer. After undressing, slowly lower the swimmer to the sitting position.

Transferring from Wheelchair to Poolside

Orthodox Lift 1

Two helpers stand one each side of the wheelchair with feet apart, facing forward; hips and knees should be bent and backs straight. The helper's hands are placed under the swimmer's thighs and as low as possible behind the back. The helpers grasp each other's wrists, making a secure cradle (Fig 20).

The helpers straighten their legs and on command move forwards to the poolside. The swimmer is lowered to the poolside by the helpers who slowly bend their hips and knees (Fig 21). A helper in

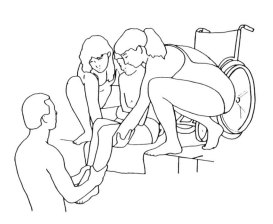

Fig 21 Slowly lowering to the poolside, bending knees to tak the weight.

Fig 20 Transfer from a wheelchair to the poolside – orthodox lift 1.

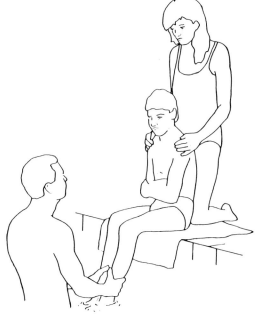

Fig 22 Supporting the swimmer on the poolside.

57

the water assists by taking the swimmer's legs and lowering them into the water, the helpers on the poolside taking an equal share of the swimmer's weight. During this lift, the swimmer's arms should be folded and the swimmer tilted slightly backwards. When the swimmer is sitting, one helper moves behind to help maintain this position (Fig 22).

Orthodox Lift 2

During this lift the swimmer's arms are placed around the two helpers' shoulders, the helpers standing on each side of the wheelchair with feet apart, facing forward. The helpers' hips and knees are bent and their backs straight. They place their hands under the swimmer's thighs and as low as possible behind the back, and grasp each other's wrists, making a secure cradle (Fig 23).

Fig 23   Orthodox lift 2. The swimmer's arms are placed around the helper's shoulders.

Fig 24   Moving forward to the poolside, protecting the legs.

The helpers straighten their legs, and on command move forwards to the poolside. The swimmer is lowered to the poolside by the helpers slowly bending their hips and knees. A helper in the water assists by taking the swimmer's legs and lowering them into the water, the helpers at the poolside taking an equal share of the weight (Fig 24).

Through Lift

Two helpers are required for the lift, and the wheelchair arm rest on one side should be removed. The swimmer should keep the elbows tucked in, if possible grasping his or her own wrists across the abdomen or chest. The first helper stands behind and to one side of the wheelchair. This helper's hands are placed under the swimmer's arms, grasping the forearms or wrists. The second helper stands to the side and with the arm rest removed supports the swimmer's thighs and lower legs (Fig 25). Both helpers stand with their hips and knees bent.

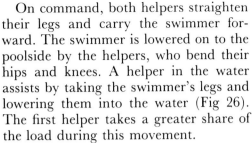

On command, both helpers straighten their legs and carry the swimmer forward. The swimmer is lowered on to the poolside by the helpers, who bend their hips and knees. A helper in the water assists by taking the swimmer's legs and lowering them into the water (Fig 26). The first helper takes a greater share of the load during this movement.

Towel Lift

A large, strong towel is slipped under the swimmer. Two helpers, facing forward, stand on each side of the wheelchair with feet apart, hips and knees bent and back straight. The helpers twist the corners of the towel to secure it around the swimmer and to create a safe grasp (Fig 27).

Fig 25   Through lift; first helper with hands under the arms, second helper supporting the thighs.

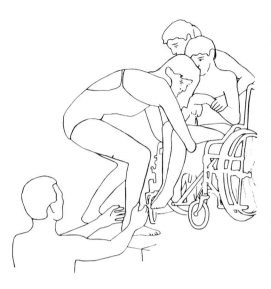

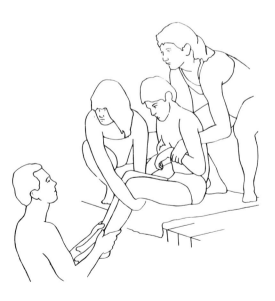

Fig 26   Through lift with helper in the water guiding the legs of the swimmer.

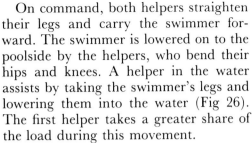

Fig 27   Towel lift; the towel corners are twisted to give a safe hold.

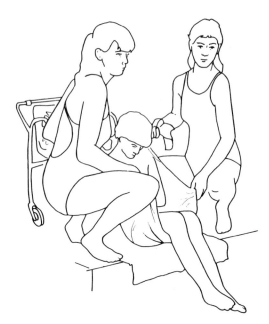

Fig 28   Towel lift, transferring to the poolside.

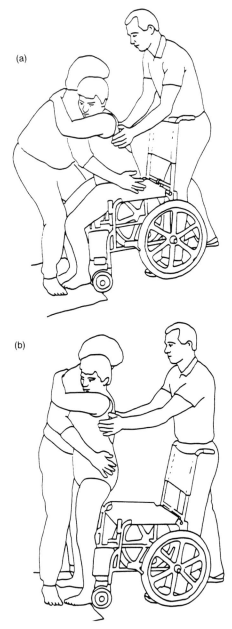

(a)

(b)

On command, the helpers straighten their legs and move forward to the poolside. The swimmer is lowered to the poolside by the helpers who slowly bend their hips and knees. The swimmer may be supported in the sitting position by remaining in the towel (Fig 28), *or* when the swimmer is sitting, one helper moves behind to help maintain this position.

Assisting Swimmer to Stand

This action involves two helpers. The swimmer's feet are positioned firmly on the ground, as close to the pool edge as is comfortable. The first helper stands to the side but facing the swimmer, blocking the swimmer's feet by placing the nearest foot against the swimmer's toes. The second helper stands behind the chair and places the hands firmly behind the

Fig 29   Assisting to stand. (a) The helper's foot is close to the swimmer's feet. (b) The swimmer is pulled/pushed into an assisted standing position.

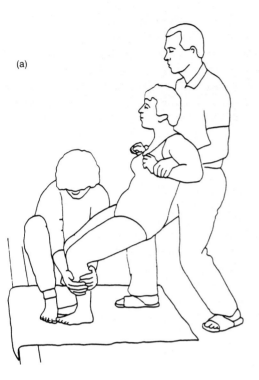

(a)

swimmer's body. The first helper then bends forward and grasps the swimmer's hips (Fig 29 (a)). On command, the swimmer is pulled/pushed into an assisted standing position. The first helper has, in the meantime, pressed the swimmer's hips forward by applying the hands to the lower spine. If possible, the swimmer should place the hands on the first helper's shoulder (Fig 29(b)).

Having wheeled the chair away, the second helper returns and stands behind the swimmer, grasping the swimmer's wrists using a through-arm grip. The first helper controls the swimmer's feet and legs by standing to the side, facing the swimmer and blocking the swimmer's feet by placing the nearest foot against the swimmer's toes. The first helper's hands support the swimmer's legs below the knees (Fig 30 (a)). On command, the swimmer is lowered to the poolside with the support of the helpers (Fig 30 (b)).

(b)

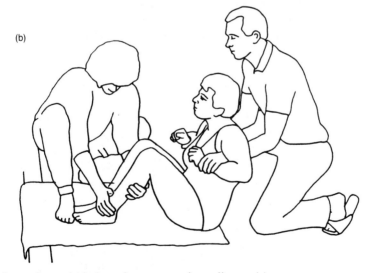

Fig 30   Lowering to the poolside from the supported standing position.
(a) The swimmer's lower legs are supported. (b) The swimmer is lowered with full support from the helpers.

Canvas Lifting Seat

The transit seat is slipped under the swimmer, a safety belt is fastened and two helpers stand one each side of the wheelchair with feet apart, facing forward. The helpers' knees and hips should be bent and their backs straight. The helpers grasp the transit handles in the orthodox manner (Fig 31).

On command, the helpers straighten their legs and move forwards to the poolside. The swimmer is lowered to the poolside by the helpers who slowly bend their hips and knees (Fig 32). The swimmer may be supported in the sitting position by remaining seated in the transit seat, *or*, when the swimmer is sitting, one helper moves behind to maintain this position.

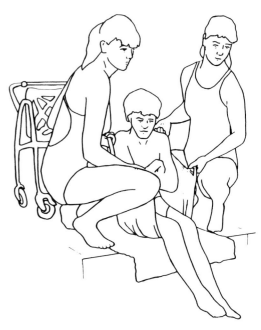

Fig 32 Supporting the swimmer on the poolside.

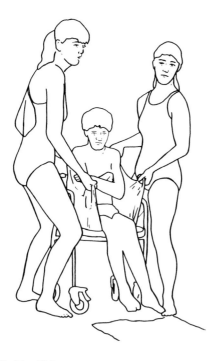

Fig 31 Using a canvas lifting seat.

Entering the Pool

It is essential that whenever possible the swimmers should be encouraged to use their own capacities for independence and mobility. Resources can often be adapted or used ingeniously to provide more independent methods of entry.

Slope or Ramp

A swimmer can shuffle down in a sitting position, depending on the floor surface. This method must *not* be used if there is a lack of sensation in the lower limbs. A shower chair can also be used with a slope or ramp. This should be taken backwards down a ramp to avoid the swimmer being tipped out or having the feet trapped.

Gently Descending Steps

These may be negotiated in a forward or backward direction. The swimmer's weaker leg should go down first, the stronger leg joining it. If necessary, the helper should stand on a lower level than the swimmer, supporting the swimmer at the hips.

Vertical Ladder

The swimmer must enter the pool facing the ladder. The swimmer's weaker leg must go down first, the stronger leg joining it. The helper should stand in the water, supporting the swimmer at the hips or guiding the feet on to the ramp.

An additional helper may be required to stand at the top of the ladder and help position and stabilise the swimmer's hands on the rails. In the case of a swimmer who is unable to use his or her hands to hold the rail of the ladder, the helper can descend the ladder in advance, whilst maintaining a very close position behind the swimmer and descending only one step ahead. The helper gives full support under the arms while holding firmly on to the rail and the swimmer is able to descend slowly and cautiously.

Swivel Entry

The swimmer sits on the side of the pool, legs hanging loosely over the edge, and the helper stands in the water. The swimmer places the hands in one of the following ways: with one hand on the pool edge, fingertips facing toward the water, reach across with the other hand, place it alongside with fingertips facing backwards; *or* place hands on the rail; *or* place hands on the rail and side. The swimmer presses down hard and turns on to his or her front, then lowers gradually into the water.

If the swimmer's arms are not strong enough to hold the head clear of the side throughout this entry, the helper should assist by holding the swimmer's hips, taking care that the swimmer's legs and abdomen do not rub on the poolside.

Corner Entry

Where the corner of the pool is clear of projections or steps this may be used by a swimmer with strong arms for an independent entry. The swimmer sits on the corner of the poolside, facing the middle of the pool and with legs hanging loosely down. With hands on the edges of the pool on each side and fingertips facing forward, the swimmer lowers into the water.

Rolling Entry

The swimmer sits on the side, rolls on to the front and enters the water.

Forward Entry with Helper

The swimmer sits as near to the poolside as is safely possible, with the feet hanging loosely over the edge. A helper may support the swimmer from behind if necessary, and another helper stands in waist-deep water with feet apart, one foot in front of the other, as close to the poolside as possible. It may be necessary to stand between the swimmer's legs or to one side (Fig 33).

The helper in the water leans forward on to the front leg and places the hands underneath the swimmer's shoulder blades. The swimmer places the hands on the helper's shoulders and moves the head forward to one side. The swimmer leans forward and is drawn into the water by the helper, who transfers weight from front to back leg and simultaneously bends the knees (Fig 34). By lowering into the water and moving backward, the helper should ensure that the swimmer's back does not rub against the poolside. The poolside helper may assist by grasping the swimmer's waist, again ensuring the swimmer's back does not rub against the poolside.

Fig 34 The helper in the water bends the knees, transferring the weight to the back leg.

Progression Supporting the Swimmer's Elbows

The swimmer sits as near to the poolside as is safely possible, with the feet hanging loosely over the edge. A helper stands in waist-deep water with feet apart, one foot in front of the other, as close to the poolside as possible. It may be necessary to stand between the swimmer's legs or to one side.

The helper in the water leans forward on to the front leg and places the hands behind the swimmer's elbows. The swimmer places the hands on the helper's

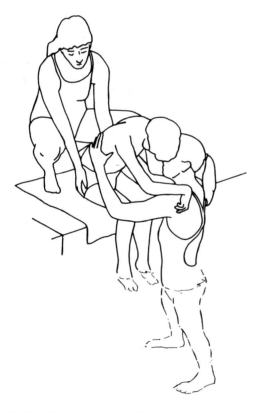

Fig 33 Forward entry 1. The helper's hands are placed underneath the swimmer's shoulder blades.

forearms and moves the head forward to one side (Fig 35). The swimmer leans forward and is drawn into the water by the helper in the water, who transfers weight from front to back leg and simultaneously bends the knees (Fig 36). The poolside helper may assist by grasping the swimmer's waist and ensuring the swimmer's back does not rub against the poolside. By supporting the swimmer's elbows and moving backward the helper in the water should also ensure that the swimmer's back does not rub against the poolside during the entry.

Fig 36   The swimmer leans forward into the water; the poolside helper protects the swimmer's back.

Progression Using Hand to Hand Support

The swimmer sits as near to the poolside as is safely possible, with the feet hanging loosely over the edge. The swimmer is supported from behind by a helper if necessary. A helper stands in waist-deep water with feet apart, one foot in front of the other, as close to the poolside as possible (Fig 37). It may be necessary to stand between the swimmer's legs or to one side. The helper in the water leans forward on the front leg and supports the swimmer's hands; the helper's palms face upward to give the required support.

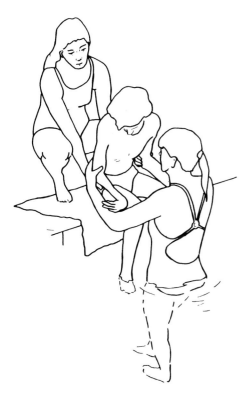

Fig 35   Forward entry 2. The helper's hands are behind the swimmer's elbows.

Fig 37   Forward entry 3, hands on hands.

The swimmer leans forward and is drawn into the water by the helper in the water, who transfers the weight from the front to the back leg and simultaneously bends the knees (Fig 38). By lowering into the water and moving backward, the helper should ensure that the swimmer's back does not rub against the poolside.

Forward Turning Entry

The swimmer sits comfortably on the poolside, legs hanging loosely over the edge. The helper stands close to the poolside in waist-deep water facing, but to the side of, the swimmer with one foot in front of the other. The helper grasps the swimmer's upper arm, holding the strong side of the swimmer with the nearer hand. The free hand is placed on the knee to stop the legs swinging (Fig 39).

Fig 38   The helper in the water moves backwards.

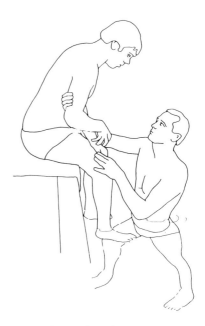

Fig 39   Forward turning entry.

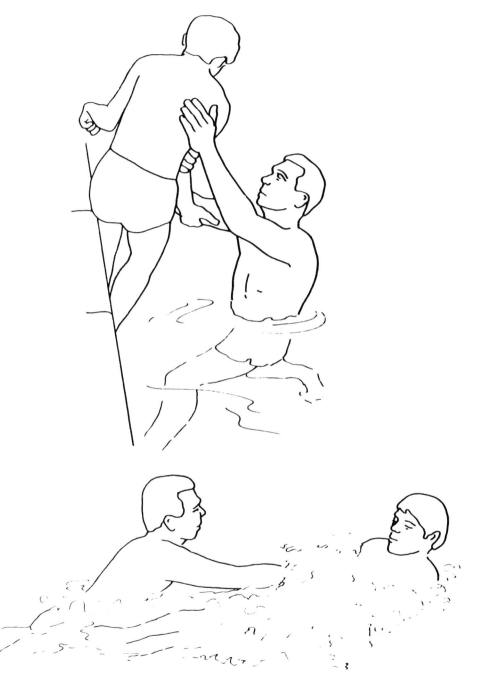

Fig 40   With shoulder leading, the swimmer enters the pool away from the side.

When the swimmer is ready, a determined head movement is made, as the body rotates and tips forward with the shoulders leading. Simultaneously, the helper pivots in the same direction, reaching round to support the swimmer across the shoulders as the swimmer lands in the water away from the poolside (Fig 40).

Orthodox and Through-Arm Grip

This lift may be used for a heavier person, or for the initial visit to the pool of someone who lacks confidence. The swimmer sits as near to the poolside as is safe, with feet hanging loosely over the edge. Two helpers stand facing each other in the water close to the swimmer and with their feet apart. The helpers' hands are placed under the swimmer's thighs and as low as possible behind the back (Fig 41). The helpers grasp each others' wrists and straighten together, then bend their knees to lift the swimmer clear of the poolside and into the water.

Sitting Lift and Towel Hoist

For a very heavy swimmer who is unable to enter the water independently an orthodox lift as already described (*see* page 57) may be used, with additional support provided by using a towel hoist and one or two extra helpers. A well-synchronised lift means three or four helpers share the weight of such a swimmer.

To perform this lift, a large strong towel or roller towel is threaded behind the swimmer's back and through under the arms; the towel is then held by one or

Fig 41   Orthodox and through-arm grip. The helpers are standing close to the swimmer.

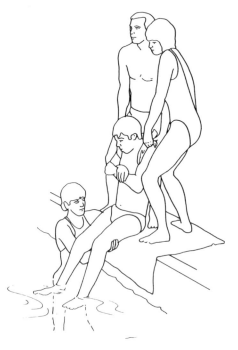

Fig 42   Sitting lift and towel hoist.

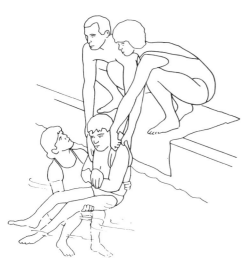

Fig 43   Helpers ensure the swimmer's back and head clear the pool edge.

two helpers standing on the poolside (Fig 42). The helpers on the poolside must bend their knees and keep their backs straight when taking the weight of the swimmer. Great care must be taken to ensure that the swimmer's back and head clear the pool edge (Fig 43).

Three-Man Lift

This lift provides total assistance to a swimmer who is unable to sit upright and who lacks confidence or independence. The swimmer is lowered to a supine position on the poolside, parallel to the edge and as close to the side as is safely possible. Three helpers in the water stand facing the swimmer, close to the wall with their feet apart and one foot in front of the other. The first helper stands opposite the swimmer's shoulders and extends the arms under the swimmer's head and shoulders, the second helper stands opposite the swimmer's hips and extends the arms underneath and either side of the swimmer's hips, with the palms down, and the third helper stands opposite the swimmer's knees and supports the lower legs (Fig 44).

On command, the helpers lift the swimmer as if on a platform. The helpers step back simultaneously from the poolside and, by bending their knees, slowly lower the swimmer into a supine position in the water (Fig 45).

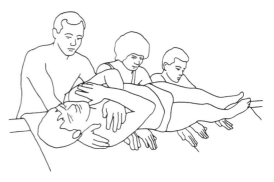

Fig 44   Three-man lift.

Fig 45   The swimmer is lowered to a supine position in the water.

69

Three-Man Roll

If a swimmer is able to roll sideways, this variation is more appropriate than the lift. A mattress which hangs over the edge of the pool is essential for comfort during this entry. The helpers and the swimmer should be positioned as for the three-man lift (see above). When ready, the swimmer turns the head towards the water and rolls towards the helpers who simultaneously raise their palms to assist the roll. They then step back and sink down into the water, supporting the swimmer. As the swimmer increases in confidence the roll may be executed with less assistance, and finally independently.

With this entry, and with the three-man lift, care should be taken to watch for trailing arms. If possible, the swimmer should fold the arms across the chest.

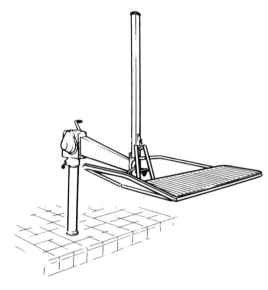

Fig 46   Mechanical pool lift.

Mechanical Hoists

Mechanical hoists should be used when:

● Human assistance is not sufficiently strong or safe.
● There are not enough helpers.
● Very heavy people are being lifted.
● Helpers have to lift many people during the day.

Dependence on this type of aid should be avoided, and those who are introduced to the pool using a hoist should be encouraged to choose more independent means of entry as their confidence grows.

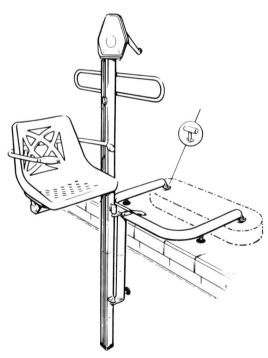

Fig 47   Mechanical pool chair hoist.

Exits from the Pool

Many of the actions used for assisted entries may be reversed. It must be remembered, however, that lifting against the pull of gravity is more difficult.

Slope or Ramp

Some swimmers can move along a slope or ramp by shuffling in a sitting position. Alternatively, a shower chair can be used, but it should be taken up backwards to avoid trapping the swimmer's feet. An extra helper standing in front of the chair may be required, to support the swimmer.

Steps

A forward exit with the stronger leg leading is sometimes possible, if necessary with a helper supporting the hips from behind.

Vertical Ladder

A forward exit is possible with the stronger leg leading. The helper stands behind and guides the swimmer's feet on to the rungs to prevent injury. As with this method of entry, the helper may ascend the steps directly behind the swimmer in order to give firmer support. An additional helper may also stand at the top of the steps to guide the swimmer's hands and provide extra support if required.

Corner Exit

This method may be used by a swimmer who has strong arms, in a pool which has rails or where there is not too great a height from the pool edge to the water.

The swimmer's back is positioned into the corner of the pool. The swimmer bends the elbows behind and places the hands on the rail or on the poolside. The swimmer levers up to a sitting position on the corner of the poolside.

Lifting

Many of the actions for lifting entries involving more than one helper can be reversed for the exit provided the helpers are strong enough. In some instances, an additional helper may need to be involved. When lifting a swimmer from the pool, the upthrust of the water should be exploited to reduce the gravitational pull. One, two or three helpers will be required in the water depending on the size of the swimmer.

The swimmer lies near to and parallel with the pool wall with the arms, if possible, folded across the chest. A heavy adult swimmer will require three helpers who stand alongside, facing the swimmer and the wall. The helpers stand close to the swimmer and place their arms under the body to form a cradle as in the three-man lift. The swimmer should be comfortable and relaxed. The helpers stand with one foot in front of the other, hips and knees bent and back straight.

The swimmer is 'bounced' up and down in the water, taking care not to submerge the head. On the third count, the helpers straighten their knees and the swimmer is lifted above the height of the wall and lowered gently on to the poolside. The helpers then leave the water to assist the swimmer into a sitting position and then a wheelchair.

Facing the Poolside

In this exit, the swimmer faces and places both hands on the poolside, then pushes with the arms and straightens the elbows to lift the upper body sufficiently to lie over the poolside. A helper standing in the water may assist by lifting the swimmer's hips.

The swimmer then wriggles further on to the poolside so that the hips are moved over the edge. A helper may assist by lifting from behind. The swimmer rolls over on to the back; a helper can assist by crossing the swimmer's legs in the direction of the roll. The swimmer rises to a sitting position. Assistance is provided by a helper standing sideways to the poolside, and reaching across to grasp the swimmer's opposite wrist with one hand while holding down the legs with the other hand, then pulling the swimmer up.

Methods of Handling in the Water

As all swimmers are unique, helpers must be ready to adapt and alter techniques according to each person's needs. The only 'correct' methods are those which suit the individual swimmer. Many people, especially those with severe impairments, will require support in the water for a long time. The teacher has to decide whether this support is to be human or artificial.

Helpers involved with supporting in the water should keep their feet apart to form a firm base, and keep their shoulders submerged. Rapid movements in the water, which may lead to a loss of control, should be avoided. The helper should have a constant awareness of sudden changes in depth and take care in shallow water to avoid abrasions to the swimmer's limbs, which may be in contact with the pool floor. Confidence can be built by using a firm but not too tight grip with the swimmer. Any type of collision should be avoided.

Group Support

Group supports may be used for games activities or for the less able or more timid pupils. Where there is a ratio of one helper to one swimmer, circle or line formations result in the swimmer having a helper on each side.

Circle Formations

Cross-Arm Support

Each helper supports the swimmer on either side by extending their arms around the backs of the swimmers, grasp-

Fig 48   Circle formation with cross-arm support.

72

ing the wrist or forearm of the helper on the opposite side of the swimmer. The swimmers rest their arms on the helpers' shoulders or forearms (Fig 48). The helpers stand in the water with their feet apart, knees bent and shoulders below the surface of the water.

Through-Arm Support
Each helper supports the swimmer on either side by extending an arm under the swimmer's shoulder and grasping the wrist of the swimmer with the thumbs uppermost (Fig 49). The helper stands in the water with feet apart, knees bent and shoulders below the surface of the water.

Palm-to-Palm Support
The helper supports the swimmer on either side by holding the swimmer's palms under the surface of the water. The helper's palms face upward, with the swimmer's palms pressing down as much as is necessary (Fig 50). The helper stands in the water with feet apart, knees bent and shoulders below the surface of the water.

Line Formations

Through-Arm Support
The swimmers are positioned between the helpers, with everyone facing the same direction. The helpers extend their arms under the shoulders of the swimmer in front to grasp the waist of the next helper (Fig 51). The swimmer may hold the shoulders of the helper in front.

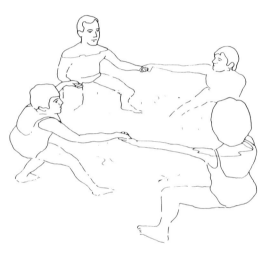

Fig 50   Circle formation with palm-to-palm support.

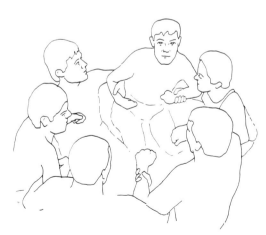

Fig 49   Circle formation with through-arm support.

Fig 51   Line formation with through-arm support, the helper's arms passing under the swimmer's shoulder to grasp the waist of the next helper.

Individual Support

Sitting

This is particularly successful with children. As the swimmer enters the water, the helper adopts a half-kneeling position. The swimmer is cradled in a side-on position across the helper's knee, and the helper places an arm around the swimmer's back, providing a comfortable and secure support (Fig 52). The other hand is free to demonstrate tasks, hold, or play (for example, washing water over the face, or picking up a toy).

Straddle

This has the advantage of face-to-face contact. It is much more reassuring, as the helper can talk to and monitor the

Fig 53   Individual support in a straddle position.

reactions of the pupil. As the swimmer enters the water, the helper bends both hips and knees and the swimmer sits astride the helper's hips. The helper supports behind the swimmer's shoulders and the swimmer places the hands on the helper's arms or shoulders (Fig 53).

Mushroom

This is useful for a timid pupil, an unco-ordinated pupil, or one who tends to 'strangle hold' by gripping the helper too tightly. As the swimmer enters the water, the helper turns the swimmer so that they both face the same direction. The helper holds the swimmer close and reaches under the arms of the swimmer to hold just below the swimmer's knees, which are bent close to the chest (Fig 54). The swimmer's arms are free to splash or scull in the water or the helper may secure the swimmer's hands or wrists over the knees.

Fig 52   Individual support in a sitting position.

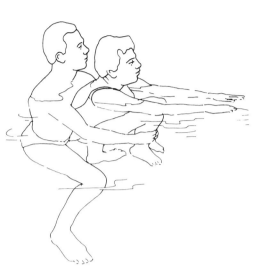

Holding a Prone Position

The helper guides the swimmer into a front floating position and reaches under the arms of the swimmer to hold on to the sides of the chest. The swimmer's arms rest on the arms of the helper (Fig 56). The helper should keep the back straight and shoulders under the water.

Fig 54   Individual support in a mushroom position.

Prone and Supine Supports

These are useful supports for adults or more nervous children in the early stages of learning to swim, as well as for people with disability. The amount of support is gradually reduced until the helper is able to move the hands momentarily out of contact with the swimmer. This stage may be reached in one lesson or it may take several years. The pupil should be made aware that the water will give support.

Holding a Supine Position

The helper guides the swimmer into a back floating position and gives support under the swimmer's hips or waist. The swimmer's head rests on the helper's shoulders (Fig 55). The helper should keep the back straight and shoulders under the water.

Fig 55   Supporting in a supine position.

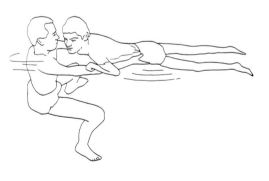

Fig 56   Supporting in a prone position.

To lift a swimmer quickly from the prone position: The helper moves very close to the swimmer and slides the hands around the swimmer's lower chest to the front, at the same time putting one leg forward, bending at the hips and knees and pushing the chest against the swimmer's head and shoulders. The helper then quickly straightens the knees, transferring the weight on to the forward leg and using the hands to bring the swimmer upward and forward to cough if necessary, and to recover.

Rolling

Many people are frightened of rolling from supine to prone, then to supine, so care should be taken that the movement is carried out smoothly and carefully, at first keeping the swimmer's face clear of the water if necessary. Ideally, a swimmer should be taught to exhale with the face submerged before this activity is introduced.

The activity should be fully explained to the swimmer before the helper proceeds. The helper then stands facing and close to one side of the swimmer, at head level, the helper's hands supporting the side of the swimmer's chest. To turn, the swimmer moves one arm across to the side away from the helper and simultaneously turns the head in the same direction (if the swimmer turns towards the helper, the helper may be struck by a fist or a shower of water). The swimmer turns to the prone position with minimal support from the helper, but initially with verbal guidance. The helper raises the swimmer sufficiently to keep the mouth clear of the water, and the swimmer turns the head and moves one arm across, so returning to the supine position. This can be repeated to the opposite side after the helper has changed position.

Turbulent Gliding

A swimmer in a supine floating position makes no propulsive movement, but is drawn through the water by the action of the helper, and moves as a result of water turbulence. The helper stands behind the head of the floating swimmer and creates a strong swirl under the shoulder blades of the swimmer through the use of a strong sculling action. As the helper moves backwards the swimmer is drawn along without contact.

When using any lifts or supports, consider carefully the ability of the swimmers, and maintain their dignity by helping only as is required. Lifting can be dangerous unless performed properly, so there is a need for supervised practice.

5   Water Activities for Parents and Children

Parent and child swimming classes have become very popular recently. This has resulted in the need for criteria to be established by which classes may be run so that they progress effectively and safely. This chapter provides a basis from which teachers of such classes may develop their own expertise.

Philosophy and General Aims

The success of parent and child classes depends upon their meeting in a comfortable, warm environment so that water activities may take place without the inhibiting discomfort of being cold and therefore miserable. Babies and toddlers need warmth and encouragement. Progress occurs when they are ready physically, mentally and emotionally, so classes must cater for individual rates of progress. Children learn by experimenting until they succeed, by watching other people in action, by being shown skills performed by someone else, and not so much by being told what to do. Below the age of three the children are learning the skills from which the ability to swim will come. Most publicised examples of newly born babies swimming have been taken in carefully monitored, clinical conditions. It is inadvisable for the teacher to experiment in such a way with

babies, or to allow them into the public pool environment until they have been immunised, which is usually completed by the age of five months.

The aims of running parent and child classes include the following:

(i)   To train the parent to guide the child so that both have respect for water and safety.
(ii)   For the child to gain confidence in the pool environment.
(iii)   For the child to gain the level of balance, propulsion and independence in water that physical and mental development allow.
(iv)   For the child to progress from independently propelling itself through the water, supported by buoyancy aids, to an ability to swim without such aids.
(v)   To offer the child an opportunity for social and emotional education, in accepting and getting to know the other people in the class and in facing the initially strange environment.

The aim of parent and child classes is to promote better water safety, to encourage social skills by parent and child interaction, to offer water activity in an atmosphere of fun, play and harmony, and to enhance the child's physical development in a healthy, stimulating environment. As such, the classes are of positive value in a child's upbringing.

Fig 57 Enjoyment.

The Development of the Young Child

A child's development consists of spurts of rapid growth followed by lulls, which are unique in timing and in extent for every child. Between the ages of five and forty-eight months, the changes in build, strength, control, awareness and attitudes are vast.

The level of ability in water skills is naturally related to developmental changes in the child, such as gaining control of limb movements, turning on to the front and the back, crawling, walking and then running, skipping and jumping. The small baby's ability to clench its fist develops into grasping, holding and manipulating objects. Back strength and flexibility improve until the natural body curves caused by the upright position appear. The weight of the head in relation to the whole body, commencing as proportionately very heavy in the baby, and gradually lessening as the child grows, is significant in the learning of water skills.

Mentally, the baby tends to accept different environments, provided that it is comfortable and that the parent is available when required. Later, the child becomes more interested in the surroundings, partially disengages from the parent, accepts other people, becomes more aware of danger, and has fears and regressions that can be overcome with the support of the parent. Speaking develops from gurgles and noises into garbled sounds which gradually improve into fluent and clear vocabulary. The average child talks quite fluently by the age of four. The rate of learning, like all other developments, depends upon individual aptitude and encouragement in the home.

Teachers and parents will, therefore, be teaching children with the following general characteristics:

(i) The baby – a disproportionately heavy head, a very basic form of body control with little control of the limbs, a lack of ability in speech.

(ii) The toddler – a body growing proportionately faster than the head. Improved body control, gripping with the hands, and propulsion from the limbs. More apprehension in the water, able to talk on a simple level.

(iii) The four-year-old – a body weight that more easily balances the head, a stronger and more flexible body, an adventurous attitude, an ability to talk more fluently.

The rate of learning water skills is less dependent on intelligence than on the strength of the feeling of self-preservation, for it is directly related to the degree of fear that the child has for water.

Babies' Development (5–24 Months)

Very small babies accept change more readily, usually enjoy the water, and do

Fig 58   Early introduction to the water.

Fig 59   An early starter with a variety of buoyancy aids.

not mind being briefly totally immersed. Although babies introduced to the pool at over ten months tend to show apprehension, they soon begin to enjoy the water. Babies who initially float in a supine position will only be happy in the prone position once they have learned to turn over and crawl on the floor. Water activities should not begin before the baby is able to hold up its head without help, although minimal support may still be necessary. Swimming any distance should be avoided because of the strain on bone and muscle. Children of this age are inquisitive and observant, and develop physically during the stages of crawling, standing and walking.

Toddlers' Development (24–28 Months)

Children starting to swim at two years or older are more cautious than babies and need plenty of encouragement. They take spoken advice and respond positively to praise. The child must want to acquire the new skill, either to please its parents, the teacher, or for its own gratification. Formal commands may create an adverse reaction. Skills are more easily acquired if the child sees others performing them.

During this stage of development, children are more adventurous. The muscles, bones and spinal curves are better formed. They are able to sustain their efforts for longer periods. They love to practise skills, they have more accurate body awareness, they have good head control, and they learn to progress in water in the horizontal position, responding to spoken guidance. When the toddler is tall enough to stand in shallow water, learning to swim is made easier. In this respect, shallow and 'beach' style pools are a better environment for teaching small children to swim than the conventional type of pool. After the age of three children will begin to swim without support.

Philosophy Related to Development

Babies and toddlers must be taught in a way that allows them to progress at their own individual pace. The child/parent one-to-one situation makes this possible. The parent should be trained to allow the child to experiment freely whilst being ready to give support when the child requires it. Some children appear to play aimlessly and yet are actually learning, controlling or accumulating a skill. There will be the need for some directed work during each lesson for skills which may not come naturally, such as kicking the legs in the horizontal plane.

The Role of the Parent

Parents who lack water confidence or are over-protective must not transmit their fear to the child, either through the expression in the eyes, over-quick response to the child's insecurity, or even in holding the child too firmly. The parent may find it difficult to allow the child to experiment because of the natural parental urge to protect it.

Fig 60   Happy, confident support.

Parents should be neither too protective nor too distant, both physically and mentally, and at all times sensitive to the needs of the child. The child must feel that it can rely on the parent totally. The parent should at the same time promote a feeling of freedom and adventurous investigation so that the child will move away on its own, perhaps for the first time in its life. In this situation, the parent should be close at hand, watching and ready to give support if required.

Although the parent should be ready to provide support, grabbing at the child quickly should be avoided. A firm, smooth, deliberate support should be provided only until the apprehensive expression on the child's face clears. Should the child choke on a mouthful of water, give it a soothing cuddle and send it off again. Over-fussing emphasises the problem too much in the child's mind. However, the parent should not force a child's progress too quickly. Both old and newly acquired skills need to be practised over and over again. The competitiveness of some adults is rarely echoed by children, who need to play and learn at a pace that is natural to them. Conversely, the parent must beware of restricting progress.

The parent is the main source of skill learning for the child, who observes and copies in order to learn. The parent, therefore, should swim with the child, using the actions that the child is learning. Preferably, support should be attained by the child holding on to the parent's finger, costume or arm rather than the parent holding the child. This may enhance the feeling of floating and, more importantly, the knowledge of how to hold on. The parent does not know the moment when the child is ready to let go, and thus may unwittingly inhibit the progress of the child by using continuous support.

The Role of the Teacher

The teacher has overall responsibility for the class and must ensure the safety of its participants whilst providing an ideal learning environment. In this one-to-one situation, where each parent is responsible for its child, the teacher can enter the water to give direct and individual advice to parents. It is for this reason that many of the following suggestions are parent-centred, so that the teacher may judge what advice to give according to the situation. A paired, caring group where parents look out for each other is advisable in case a parent gets into difficulty. Safety apparatus must be at hand, as well as a life-guard on the poolside. Children respond better to direct contact than to seeing the teacher shouting from the side. Parents can talk more easily to the teacher if they are near, without having to shout above background noise, and they usually prefer individual contact whilst still preferring to be directed in what to do. Parents should be encouraged to use their own initiatives within the guidelines previously provided by the teacher.

The teacher has to be cheerful, sympathetic and competent without being bossy. Reaction to dangerous behaviour or disobedience should be firm. The teacher must protect the rest of the class, even as a last resort by requesting that the offender be removed from the pool.

The teacher should aim to make swimming lessons happy, enjoyable and exciting adventures. Good rapport between teacher, parent and child is essential. Children like to recognise and focus on at least one person other than their parent amongst all of the strangers. The teacher fills this position, particularly as help is given in lifting the children into and out of the pool, and because parents turn to the teacher for advice.

Children like to be spoken to in a sunny, interested way, to be asked questions and to be given time to answer. The teacher ought to show friendliness and interest in the child as a person, avoid talking about them to their parents in a negative way whilst the children are listening, and not to be either too serious or too loud. The acceptance of the teacher by the parent may ease contact with the child.

Children enjoy play, so the teacher should pat the water, wiggle a finger up from under the water, push a ball to the child to be pushed back, push the ball under to let it 'pop' up, or any similarly shared activity. If the child shows distress in the teachers's presence, it is advisable to look away without moving away, whilst talking easily and quietly to the parent. If the child shows no reduction in fear, try moving away, allowing time for the teacher to be accepted as a familiar figure in the class. Later, try approaching again. The teacher should not force company on to children except when lifting them into or out of the pool. Physical contact ought to be gentle, yet firm and safe. The hands should feel friendly and sympathetic, the movements should be smooth and controlled, and the teacher should look at and smile at the child.

Objectives

The child should be encouraged to attain the following objectives:

● Accept immersion of the body, including water into the ears and eyes.
● Float with armbands independent of the parent in the vertical, prone and supine positions.

Fig 61   Attempting to develop propulsive actions.

- Gain and retain balance in the water, and turn at will.
- Exclude water from the nose and mouth.
- Gain water confidence.
- Accomplish propulsion with the legs.
- Move away independently from the parent.
- Accomplish propulsion with the arms as well as with the legs.
- Gradually reduce dependence upon artificial support.
- Jump into the water from the side.
- Dive from the side into deep water.

The objectives may not be attempted or attained in this order, depending upon the individual attributes and aspirations of the child.

Overcoming Fear

The parent, who is the child's haven of safety, should appear keen, happy and smiling, and be readily available at all times. Most children will enter the pool without much fuss, but all will need some degree of help and personal confidence. Only give the support that is necessary. A watering can or cup to play with may help the apprehensive child to gain in confidence. If the child clings tightly to the parent and cries continually, the parent must decide whether or not to continue. The teacher should explain that leaving the pool will not remove the problem and may even emphasise a fear of water. This fear is usually overcome if the parent is prepared to persevere with the child. The reason for fear is not always apparent and may be the result of a number of causes; for instance, the teacher may appear frightening to the child. Allow the child to overcome its fears by facing up to them itself, even if it takes weeks. Familiarity and observing other children enjoying the water overcomes most children's apprehension in time.

The very frightened child needs special help. The parent can cuddle the child whilst sitting and watching, so the child can become used to the environment and observe the other children at play. If changed, the child might wear arm bands to get used to them, although this is best done at home beforehand. Parent and child gradually move closer to the pool, walking along the side and looking at what the class is doing. The parent may enter the pool at the next lesson, and perhaps with the help of the teacher, encourage the child to join in. If the child still cries when carried in the arms of the parent, walk about in the water, talking to the child and to other people, whilst gradually lowering the child little by little into the water. Hold the child firmly yet sympathetically whilst playing with a toy such as a watering can. The parent should lower him or herself into the water with the child, meanwhile interesting the child in toys and the other swimmers.

A regression in learning or an increase in apprehension may be caused by missing a week, an illness, progressing too quickly through the skills, or something that is nothing at all to do with the pool. When this occurs, it is advisable to be patient, retreat a few stages and try again. Regression is a natural occurrence and is to be expected.

Fig 62   Play helps familiarisation with the strange environment.

The Environment

The child should wear well-fitted arm-bands or a similarly buoyant form of support if it is to feel safe in the pool; it needs to feel comfortable, warm and safe if it is to gain maximum benefit from lessons. The age range of the class will depend upon local circumstances. Younger children learn through contact with older children, but the very young can be frightened by the vigorous and boisterous actions of the bigger children.

Noise, expanse of water, strangers, lights, reflections, the ceiling, and water in the ears and eyes may all cause apprehension and fear. This fear stems from the fact that the situation is unfamiliar, and will reduce as the surroundings become more familiar. The child should not be *over* protected.

The Pool

It is essential that the water is very warm, 82°–90°F (28°–32°C), and that the surrounding air and the changing rooms are two or three degrees warmer. Water purification must be faultless. The pool should be large enough to accommodate comfortably the class of the size envisaged, and sufficiently shallow for the parents to be able to stand whilst teaching. An overall depth of one metre (3ft 3in) is ideal, especially if there is a gentle slope, or stepping, at one side. Surrounds should be wide enough to allow unrestricted movement. Exclusive use of the pool avoids distraction, unwelcome interference, embarrassment for the parents and turbulent water that may distress the babies. Seats or benches for visitors, such as grandparents, and hooks or hangers for towels and gowns, could be provided.

Changing Rooms

These must provide adequate room for the class to change in comfort, with chairs, benches and tables so that the parents may lay down changing mats. A safe locker system avoids problems with tiny clothes. Similar provision is required for the fathers who may accompany their children. Sufficient toilets, showers and facilities for washing are required, with containers for disposable nappies. Mops and buckets should be available in case of mishap. Play-pens or baby chairs allow parents to dress unhindered by the baby. A suitable push-chair rack relieves dressing room congestion.

Equipment

If possible, arrange for the storage of equipment, unless it is all provided by the pool authority. It is wise to encourage parents to provide their own armbands, with the childrens' names clearly written on them in waterproof ink for identification purposes. This also allows the teachers to speak to the children by name. Some spare armbands should be available, just in case personal ones are left at home. Armbands with two parallel air chambers, one outside the other, that encircle the arm are preferable. Coloured balls of various sizes, floats, rubber quoits and inflatable toys are useful aids. A battery-run cassette player playing suitable music will provide a pleasant background to the lesson. Mats may make entry from the poolside more comfortable. Emergency equipment such as poles should always be present on the poolside.

Fig 63   Some toys and buoyancy aids.

Hygiene

The changing rooms and the pool surrounds must be immaculate, with sani/nappy bins provided and adequate shower and washing facilities. Incontinent babies should wear plastic pants with elasticated legs. Faecal matter is unpleasant and unhygienic in the pool, and a scoop for 'accidents' must be on the poolside. Parents should be advised not to wear make-up during, nor to use baby oil on themselves or the baby before, lessons in the pool.

Preparation at Home

A pre-pool meeting of parents and teacher is advisable, where the teacher can talk on all aspects of the lesson and safety, perhaps show a video on teaching babies, hand out relevant leaflets and tell the parent how to prepare the baby for the swimming pool. The strangeness of the swimming pool may be difficult for the baby to accept, so training at home beforehand will be helpful. The aim of pre-training is to familiarise the baby with several aspects of the pool environment, including the buoyant property of water, moving in the water, swimming aids, the supportive role of the parent, and the enjoyment of water activity.

Commence training in the baby bath, with the water deep enough to cover the ears when the baby lies down, whilst keeping the face exposed. Increase the depth as the baby develops skill, such as arm-deep water if the baby can support itself whilst floating on the surface. Gradually reduce the bath water temperature until it matches that of the swimming pool.

Activities in the Bath

Support baby horizontally in the supine position by providing support under the head/neck and seat (Fig 64). Support the baby in the prone position by providing support under the chest and hips (Fig 65). Talk, sing and generally play with the baby, making use of floating toys. The baby may only require head support, as its body will float. Reduce support as balance, skill and relaxation develop. Encourage experimentation with movements of the body and limbs. Initially, gentle forward and backward movements in the water may soothe a baby's qualms. Sprinkle water over the head with a sponge to prepare for water on the face. Create small waves and allow them to flow around baby's head in the direction of the feet. Accompany this with bubble-blowing into the water to suggest blowing out under water. If water flowing around and over the head does not worry the baby, attempt full submersion for a few moments. Always support the baby so that free arm move-

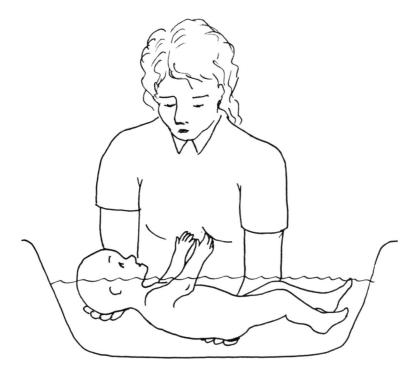

Fig 64   Supine position – support under the head and seat.

Fig 65   Prone position – supporting under the chest and hips.

ment is possible. When ready, take baby into the family bath with you, and eventually without you.

Introduce floating toys, coloured balls, quoits and other suitable objects, so that when the pool lessons begin the baby takes along a toy that is familiar. Familiarity with buoyancy aids, such as armbands, will help the settling in process because they can be restricting and thus initially frightening. Introduce them first as floating toys, and later as buoyancy aids. Very small children tend to accept them more readily than those over eight months. Although armbands do restrict arm movements, particularly for very small babies, they allow safe freedom of movement independent of the parent. Snugly fitting inflatable rings allow free movement of the limbs but, as explained later, a child can float in them upside-down.

The parent should be within easy reach of the baby in the bath so that full control and positive support are immediately available. The baby's head should be protected at all times. Babies that feel secure are more likely to become adventurous. The parent must be prepared to let go if the baby wishes it, whilst still being ready with support if required. At this stage, good judgement is necessary.

The First Visit to the Pool

As mentioned, a baby faces new and sometimes strange experiences on its first visit. The teacher and the parent should avoid anxiety through a friendly, sensitive yet firm approach to supplement the pre-pool preparation. For success, the occasion should be a happy one, and a preliminary visit to the pool is strongly recommended. Be prepared to change into swimsuits straight away if the child is willing or only a little unsure.

Put on the armbands, snugly fitting, at the top of the arms. When the teacher is ready in the pool, carry the baby and pass it down with its back to the teacher. Climb down the steps and reclaim the baby. This will give the teacher a chance to establish some trust, and in time the baby will go to the teacher willingly.

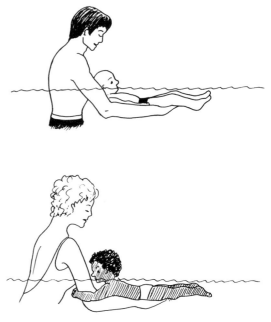

General Support

At first, the child should be supported so that its head and neck are above the water. When the child has more confidence, only the head should be raised, with the chin resting on the water. Support the body with hands under the chest and tummy, or standing beside the

Fig 66   Supporting the child under the body.

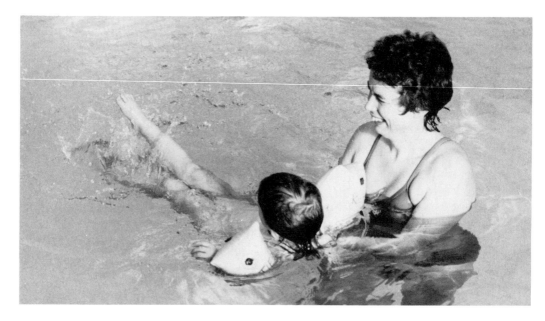

Fig 67   Standing beside the child.

child, with hands round the chest, fingers under and forward and thumbs on top. Allow the child to feel itself floating, providing only sufficient support to let the child feel safe. Holding the child under the chin may strain the neck and constrict blood vessels, so let the child hold up its own head.

Artificial Aids

Armbands restrict both vision and arm movements, yet they offer something more important, which is individual freedom. Using a ring around the body leaves the arms free, but it can be dangerous because the child may fall out or even turn upside-down. If used, a ring should be firmly strapped on. Costumes, which have pockets to hold polystyrene floats,

Fig 68   Polyotter suit on a three-year-old child.

Fig 69   Introduction of a float prior to removing arm bands (2½ years).

91

leave the arms free but young babies are too small for them, and they are of more use after the child has reached 24 months. Good armbands offer freedom, because the child feels secure and the head is held clear of the water. They are worn up close to the shoulders, with the inflation nozzles pushed in and no sharp corners near the eyes. The two armbands must give equal floatation for stability

Allow independent floatation, for parental support at this stage restricts progress. Let the children float vertically, prone or supine, as they wish. As they gain in skill and confidence, let a little air out of the outside chamber of the armband. The inner chamber prevents the armband from slipping off. Decide on this the week before so that the child enters the water with the support already reduced. A reduction during the lesson may unnerve the child. Reduce the air by a quarter each time, sufficient to encourage the child to support itself more effectively. When the outside chamber is empty, cut if off, thus permitting freer arm movements. Continue to reduce the air in the armbands until the child is swimming unaided. Hand-held floats may be introduced before dispensing totally with the armbands.

The Lesson

The lesson should be conducted in an orderly manner with all reasonable precautions taken for the safety of the class. A 10 minute lesson should be sufficient for a child new to the pool, gradually extending to 20 minutes or longer for the confident children. Try to end the lesson when the child is happy and wanting to continue, and never let the children become cold and miserable. Form classes by age so that the babies of five to 30 months are separated from the toddlers of 31 to 48 months.

The class may be taken as a whole. However, the one-to-one situation makes individual tuition possible. The variations between children's rate of growth and speed in learning skills, the need for parents to come and go as individual feeding and sleeping times dictate, and the turnover in members of the class, makes individual tuition preferable. However, individual tuition makes great demands on the teacher and a novice may find teaching the class as a whole easier at first.

The teacher trains the parents by setting general tuitional guidelines through which to attain objectives. The teacher then advises the parent how to progress, through observation of the individual child's development in watermanship, independence and readiness to progress. At first the child learns by experimenting, discovering what works best and copying. Later, explanations will help learning. At the end of the lesson, allow the child a few minutes to enjoy the freedom of being without armbands, to experience a real sense of floatation.

Parents should not be allowed to look after two children at once in the pool for reasons of safety, unless one of them can move quite confidently and independently in the water. The teacher should assess the situation carefully because jealousy may cause the confident child to cling for attention.

Lesson Format

1 Prepare for the lesson:
Teacher: apparatus, personal clothing.

Fig 70   A variety of activities encouraged by parents.

Parent: change, warm towel and gowns near the poolside, artificial aids on and checked, toys ready.

2   Enter the pool.

3   Re-introduce the child to the water and the teacher.

4   The teacher should provide individual advice and teaching from initial observation.

5   Armbands should be taken off for the last minutes of the lesson. This may be extended if the child is tall enough to stand in the shallow end or if there is a gradual slope down into the water.

6   Leave the pool, put on a warm towel or gown and change.

Class Procedure

On Arrival

(i)   A procedure for signing in will assist the teacher to check attendance, remember names and to record progress.

(ii)   A 'park' for pushchairs avoids obstruction and dirt.

(iii)   No one with infectious or contagious diseases, colds or sores should attend classes.

(iv)   Storage facilities and a method of identifying belongings are advisable.

(v)   Adherence to the rules of hygiene is essential.

Preparation by the Teacher
(i) Safety equipment should be readily available and accessible.
(ii) Teaching aids should be checked and placed at convenient points around the pool. The music should be ready to be switched on.

Preparation on the Poolside
Ideally, chairs and benches should be available so that parents may sit down to fit armbands. Parents who have previously attended a class may take their babies into the pool on the direction of the teacher. Newcomers should remain on the poolside in order to observe safe methods of entry and be advised on safe methods of procedure generally. It is recommended that the teacher does not enter the water, unless a suitably qualified assistant is in attendance on the poolside, even though direct contact is preferable. The teacher should be summoned immediately in the event of danger, and a single blast on the whistle meaning 'move to the nearest side of the pool' should be taught to the class and immediately obeyed.

Leaving the Pool
(i) Leave the pool when the child is happy. Shivering babies should be taken out, wrapped in a towel and kept warm.
(ii) Collect personal belongings, such as armbands, to avoid having to return to the pool.
(iii) Drying and dressing should be completed quickly and thoroughly.
(vi) Place the baby in the high chair/play-pen whilst the parent is dressing.
(v) A biscuit or drink away from the poolside may help the baby settle down.
(vi) Before leaving the premises, parents should check their belongings and dispose of any litter. The teacher can inform parents of handouts that may be available and where to obtain them. Finally, the teacher should check that all poolside equipment is stored correctly.

Activities

Most of the activities with babies in the water are initiated by the babies themselves, which is to be encouraged in this 'find out by experimenting' form of education. The parent and the teacher provide the environment so that the baby is guided in its explorations, guidance being in the form of contrived situations and demonstrations.

Under Twelve Months

(i) The parent cradles the baby in the arms, lowers it into the water with minimal support and rocks it gently backwards and forwards, talking to it soothingly. At first the parent should avoid water washing over its face.
(ii) The parent gradually withdraws support until the baby floats free, supported by armbands only. The parent should keep hands close underneath the baby at first, making slight touches now and again on the baby's back for its reassurance. The baby should be able to see and hear the parent at all times until it makes its own attempt to focus elsewhere. Wet baby's hair by dribbling a handful of water over the head.
(iii) Allow the baby the freedom to experiment independently. Every little movement made by the baby in the water is an experiment in balance, control or propulsion. Allow time for experimenting. The child may lose its balance and

Fig 71   Using a toy to encourage movement.

swing over and round; give it time to regain balance itself, and only give support if there is obvious difficulty. Movements may include pushing the feet up and forwards to the supine position, swinging to the vertical and thence to the prone position, at the same time turning round and moving along.

(iv)   The baby will teach itself to swing the feet forward, bend its hips to regain the vertical, arch its back into the prone position, and bend the knees to regain the vertical.

(v)   The response of the baby in the water depends on its development of skill on land. When it is very young (five or six months) it is quite content to lie on its back in the water. When it turns over on land, it is also happier lying prone in the water. When it learns to crawl, it tries to crawl in the water and gains a little propulsion. When it can walk upright it prefers to swim with a walking (cycling) action in the water.

(vi)   Very small babies are likely to use a simultaneous kick directly backwards for propulsion, rather like a dolphin action.

(vii)   Encourage the baby to turn its head by going behind it and calling. Later it may be supplemented by a body twist and then by arm propulsion to turn round completely. Encourage it to reverse direction. In time the baby will learn to spin round.

Under Twenty-Four Months

(i) The baby may find it difficult to kick its legs horizontally on the surface until it is older. It finds a vertical position from which to control the proportionately heavy head easier. This reduces the strain on the neck caused by holding the head back.

(ii) Allow time for the baby to observe other people, the rail, the steps and the water. The baby learns by copying other people as well as the parent.

(iii) Use toys as an attraction to encourage propulsion. Place one just out of the baby's reach and encourage it to move towards and to grasp the toy. Similarly, allow them to explore the rail, the steps and, particularly, other babies and parents.

(iv) It is natural for babies to drink the water (and well nigh impossible to stop them). Let them learn to prevent water from entering the mouth or to spit it out once it has entered, rather than protecting them from coughing and spluttering. Teach bubble blowing so that they find out that it is a good way of repelling water.

(v) From a sitting position on the poolside, the baby can be lifted down into the water, with a 'One, two, three – Weeeee!' In time, this may develop into a jump with minimal or no support.

(vi) Hold the baby firmly in the arms and go under for a short period. This is humorously referred to as 'dunking'. Count out loud 'One, two, three!', blow into the baby's face, and when it has taken a breath, go under. Come up laughing and talking to reassure the baby. Do this only two or three times per lesson.

(vii) Other activities may include:

● Pulling the baby prone or supine through the water.
● The baby riding on the parent's back or tummy.
● Bobbing up and down in the water – games such as 'ring-a-ring-a-roses', 'humpty-dumpty', 'the big ship sails through the alley-alley-oo', 'pop goes the weasel'.
● Lifting baby up into the air, releasing and then immediately catching it with great care.
● Baby riding on an inflated toy.
● Baby travelling hand-over-hand along the bar.
● Introducing a reward to encourage swimming for short distances.

Under Thirty-Six Months

The activities practised with babies continue into the toddler age group with modifications according to physical and mental development. Similarly, many of the activities mentioned below may be used in the baby group.

(i) Splashing games – with ball, quoit, toy, parent or baby.

(ii) Ball games – pat, push, push under, pass to parent with the hand, forehead or nose.

(iii) Playing independent of the parent.

(iv) Insist that the child has to fetch anything that it wants.

(v) The parent moves away, calls the child and stands still until the child arrives.

(vi) Demonstrate 'dog paddle' to the child, with emphasis on the arms to encourage their use.

(vii) Blow bubbles under water and make funny noises. Encourage the child to do the same.

Fig 72   Lifting out of the water.

Fig 73   Action song.

Fig 74   Following mummy and brother.

(viii) Continue with the 'dunking' exercise.

(ix) Draw the child through the water by the hands, head first, either prone or supine. The child usually enjoys the flow of water and thus may be encouraged to swim. The child may hold hands with the parent, or hold their costume or neck. Develop the activity into circles, curves and zigzags.

(x) If the child takes in too much water, cuddle it and pat the back to dislodge the water, then send it off again. Children soon learn to exclude water from the mouth.

(xi) The child takes a piggy-back ride as the parent swims along.

(xii) Use nursery rhymes and children's songs with actions for the children to take part in.

(xiii) If the toddler is moving freely, supported by armbands, the parent can encourage swimming by moving and playing close to the child.

(xiv) Guide the toddler positively towards using the legs and arms for propulsion. Lay the child between the parent's arms, head towards the parent, either prone or supine. Hold the thighs and move them vertically and alternately, simulating the crawl leg kick. Similarly, the arms and hands can be moved manually in the correct action so that the child may feel the required movement. The child will swim fast enough to maintain floatation as strength and stamina grow.

(xv) The child may be introduced to jumping from the side into the pool by the following stages:

Fig 75   First attempt at an entry from the side (2 years).

Fig 76   Jumping in, parent close by.

● The child sits on the side with feet on the rail, pointing forward. The parent lifts the child into the water, at first holding under the arms, then by the hands.
● The child sits as before and launches into the parent's arms in the pool.
● The parent allows the child to submerge in the water progressively deeper before catching it.
● The child jumps into the water and is brought to the surface by the armbands, the parent staying close at hand.
● The same activity as above, but with the child jumping from the side, commencing with the toes curled over the edge.
● The leap becomes more and more horizontal until, into water of 1½ metres

(4ft 11in), it becomes a dive. Ensure that there is sufficient depth of water for the size of the child.
(xvi)   Allow the child to enjoy repeating familiar movements, as long as they are performed correctly. Children are happy repeating their achievements.

Under Forty-Eight Months

(i)   As the support required from the armbands becomes minimal, encourage the child to spend more and more time without them. The parent's arm may be used as a 'rail' whilst the child is kicking across the pool. Alternatively, a bar-type aid will give some support and encourage movement. Kicking at a stationary rail soon becomes boring.
(ii)   Encourage the advanced children to swim without armbands, especially if they are able to recover their feet. If one child begins to swim, the others are sure to follow suit. It may be worth giving an advanced group extra attention to get them swimming.
(iii)   The parent and child should spend more and more time in going under water and playing, so that the fear of total immersion is dispelled.
(iv)   The parent and the teacher stand a short way apart and push the child to each other through the water, encouraging it to swim. Observation will tell how far the child is able to swim, and the distance between the adults can be increased gradually as long as the child improves.
(v)   The float can be introduced now, with a demonstration of how to hold it and what to do. It is wise for the parent to stay close as the child is likely to let go of the float suddenly.
(vi)   Children may be put off by formal

Fig 77   Independent jump (3 years).

Fig 78   Holding a bar-type aid.

commands, so encourage and lead rather than order. However, it would appear sensible to insist on serious practice for some part of the lesson if the child is to progress; continuous play may become aimless.

(vii)   A badge for swimming without armbands would be a great incentive at this stage, but use the competitive urge wisely.

Toys

Toys make play easier, and a favourite toy promotes familiarity with the environment. They help the baby to forget the strangeness of the surroundings, whilst a new plaything can stimulate an inquisitiveness that supersedes fear.

Suitable toys may include the following: plastic balls of a smallish size, quoits

Fig 79   Reaching for a toy.

and other toys to grip, plastic animals, boats and ducks, inflatable animal toys, aeroplanes and balloons, and mechanical swimming toys. These may be supported by squeezy bottles, floating cups, plastic toy watering cans, rubber rafts and rings, floating watertight containers with handles, and similar objects. Bright objects that sink are useful in shallow water in order to encourage children to go under water to recover them.

Ensure that the toys are clean, non-toxic, unbreakable, light, blunt, and are neither small enough nor have parts that are small enough to go into a baby's mouth. The baby should be able to take hold of and lift the toy.

Safety

Toddlers cannot be relied upon to learn the rules of true water safety or to know how to act in an emergency. The life-guard and the teacher should both be suitably qualified in rescue techniques. They ought to know the pertinent first aid and have practised expired air resuscitation and external cardiac compression on a child dummy. Some authorities have resuscitators, but these can be a hindrance except under ideal conditions. The teacher must know the regulations for the pool in the case of an emergency, where the nearest telephone is installed, the facilities for first aid, and also the requirements of the Health and Safety Executive for swimming pools.

Despite the fact that these classes are a one-to-one situation, a parent may get into difficulties, so it is advisable to have a pairing system whereby the parents keep an eye on their partner parent. All buoyancy aids that are worn must be safe and well-fitting.

Fig 80   Holding a baby for expired air resuscitation.

Special care should be taken when the baby first tastes freedom, and particularly when the toddler takes off the arm-bands and tries to swim. When a child is jumping in, make sure that the pool is deep enough; it should be at least the child's height with arms stretched above the head. Have the child's ears medically checked to ensure that water in them is not detrimental. Also, do not let the child swallow large quantities of water. Small quantities do not affect the child, so immersing two or three times during a lesson is safe.

Life-saving and cardio pulmonary resuscitation techniques for a baby and an infant differ from those for an adult and need to be practised.

First Aid
Medical aid should be summoned in all cases of emergency. The likely emergencies are a child hitting the bottom of the pool, a child being dropped or falling

on a hard surface, and those connected with swallowing too much water. It is possible that an adult may be taken ill rather than a child.

Royal Life Saving Society examinations require the ability to check whether a casualty is breathing and the heart is beating, how to open the airway and to put a person in the recovery position. Teachers are advised to take further training in first aid so that they may know how to deal with, and recognise, cardiac arrest and other conditions that may arise, such as shock. Be prepared and be watchful, for the best-laid plans can go wrong. Young children, particularly of pre-school age, should not be considered 'water safe', and must be carefully supervised when in or around the pool. To supervise correctly is to allow not one moment of inattention.

Before taking a class, ask the parents for details of any abnormalities that may put them or their children at risk when in the swimming pool.

Organising and Administration

It is advisable to find the right environment for parent and child classes before starting recruitment. The conditions will affect success, especially the water and air temperatures. Many such classes do not flourish because the water is too cold or the changing rooms are 'freezing'. A good, co-operative relationship with the pool management will help ensure success. Exclusive use of the pool, storage for pool apparatus, furniture to aid the parents in the changing rooms, life-guard back-up, and support in other areas of safety are all matters to be decided upon.

Choose the time of the class carefully. Mornings are usually best, between 9.30 and 10.30 a.m., when the parent may be able to organise free time to attend and avoid baby's sleep and meal times.

Decide on the fee to be charged; it should be enough to enable classes to be self-supporting from the start. It is advisable to charge for the full course at the beginning. Advertise widely and give a central address/telephone number through which booking can be made. Places to display advertisements could include maternity hospitals, clinics (particicularly ante and post-natal), the local newspaper, newsagents and small post offices, and sports shops. Arrange with the latter to sell the right type of armbands for young children.

Write and print information leaflets containing all pertinent information on times, safety responsibilities, pool procedure and pool rules, and devise a receipt system for payments. Details of the parent and child, such as medical conditions, name, address, telephone number and doctor's address should also be recorded. Arrange pre-pool training sessions for the parents to support the information leaflets, to promote the development of inter-group relationships, to state aims and methods of achieving those aims, and to show videos of the sort of work that you intend to undertake.

A register should be kept through a signing-in system, and comments written on each child in a report book so that progress can be measured and suitable projected development devised. If you wish, keep a waiting list for group membership, but these can take up much valuable time and it may be best to run a 'first come, first served' system, with set times for signing on. Acquire and arrange for the storage of the right type and amount of equipment that you will need.

Although competition should not be over-encouraged, a badge system can stimulate progress, particularly among the parents. However, keep the classes sociable and invite spectators from among spouses, friends and grand-parents.

6 Teaching Special Adults in Groups

This chapter considers the teaching of swimming to those who may have special needs for only a certain period of their swimming career. Whilst it relates to exclusive groups, there will often be overlap between the groups. For instance, there will be those from ethnic minority groups in adult classes, or there will be adults with physical or sensory impairment involved in a swim for fitness programme.

Many adults will fall into the category of persistent non-swimmer, but there are some children who will, for various reasons, take much longer than their peers in learning to swim and will need to be treated as persistent non-swimmers.

Adult Groups

The teaching of swimming has traditionally related to classes of children; competitive swimmers reach peak achievement at a very early age, and swimming clubs cater for youth. This situation is changing, because many adults are now wishing to swim and are demanding a different approach from teachers. Adult non-swimmers and swimmers have special needs which the teacher, coach and leisure centre staff must recognise. Many adults are returning to swimming late in life, having been persistent non-swimmers throughout their school days. Adults turn to swimming for various reasons and form loosely into the following groups, although no groups will be exclusive:

● Non-swimmers joining a class. Some will have never swum before, but many may be classed as persistent non-swimmers.
● Those able to swim but wishing to perfect or further their skills.
● Those taking up swimming as part of a fitness programme.
● Women following an ante or post-natal water exercise programme.
● Those with permanent or temporary physical or sensory impairment for whom swimming is used for rehabilitation or as a main form of activity.
● The elderly who join a swimming group for social and psychological reasons, with less emphasis on the underlying physical benefits.

The Role of the Teacher

Most of the adult classes will be a part of non-vocational adult education which the learners attend voluntarily, so they are usually highly motivated. They know what it is they want to learn and are keen to succeed. They have maturity of outlook and many hold very strong views on how and what they should be taught.

They may complain or no longer attend if they consider the teaching or conditions inadequate. Some will be well informed, having read about the subject, watched their children in classes, or have appropriate scientific or sporting knowledge they can apply. In contrast, some will be apprehensive, unused to being taught, and have very limited physical ability. The situation presented to the teacher is challenging and very different from teaching a class of children. The final skills to be acquired may be the same but the teacher's role is very different.

The teacher should always use language suitable for an adult when talking to the swimmer, explain why an activity is being taught and give the underlying principles behind movement in water. This will promote both interest and understanding. The teacher must not only be an expert in the subject but also be able to present that knowledge in a way relevant to the group or individual. The adult should always be encouraged to greater independence of thought allied to higher standards of performance.

Maximise the contributions that social contacts within the class situation provide, as this transforms a set of individuals into a group. The teacher may at times be called upon to be a counsellor. Take full advantage of the adults' desire to learn; constantly appraise the challenge being offered, and evaluate the progress being made to sense whether the level of task is correct. Try to sort out a problem at once if there is a lack of progress. A lack of understanding by one of the class may in fact indicate that others are facing the same difficulty. The teacher may need to explain more clearly or use a different task to achieve the desired result.

Try to be very flexible in approach, as the aims of the teacher may be different from the aims and expectations of the class. Discuss with the group the plan of work, the aims of the lesson or series of lessons and mutually agree the programme. Allow a certain freedom in arriving and leaving during the lesson without causing disruption. Working at an individual pace should be encouraged, once a task has been set to cater for the wide range of physical ability, stamina and level of concentration. Individual progress must be constantly evaluated and discussed with the swimmers. Ensure that suitable facilities are available, such as warm water, privacy for changing, a variety of apparatus, refreshment or social area, and a baby minding area.

Watermanship Programme

Adult teaching should follow the stages outlined in chapter 3 to develop balance, buoyancy, confidence under water, breathing and movement. However, there are certain factors which are particular to adult learners.

Adults work well with a partner, and some will prefer partner support to buoyancy aids, whereas some will require both. The teacher should guide the use of support to ensure the swimmer has a comfortable, balanced position in the water. Partner support can, for instance, assist the swimmer to stand up from a prone or supine glide. A partner walking ahead of a swimmer as early strokes are attempted gives confidence to launch out and also to continue across the pool. Adults accept responsibility for each others learning, and they will observe and correct, given teacher guidance,

Fig 81   Hands under the shoulder blades to give support to
swimmers uncurling to a supine float.

which helps their own understanding of a skill. They will also challenge each other to attempt a new activity. The teacher must check that working with a partner is used with discretion and that both participants fulfil the swimming task; it is not one helper and one swimmer, but an equal partnership.

Adults will often establish a favourite way of moving when first learning to swim, choosing to be prone or supine, and gaining propulsion from a chosen limb action. The teacher should set a task which permits this variety of response,

such as travelling using a leg action, and then give individual help as the swimmers respond to the task in their own ways.

Floating, sculling, rotating and treading water are important safety skills which should be constantly practised, along with changing from prone to supine positions and changing direction. These skills will soon enable the swimmers to go out of their depth and be able to cope without stress should they swallow water or bump into another swimmer. Adults enjoy working to music,

Fig 82   The helper moves backwards, keeping shoulders low in the water to give support to the swimmer.

which helps them to relax, particularly at the end of a lesson when free activity can be encouraged.

Individual methods of teaching should be adopted throughout. Some adult beginners benefit from using flippers to give initial propulsion. Their use must be strictly supervised. The swimmers should be instructed to propel themselves carefully to the side of the pool to rest, as standing up when wearing flippers is very difficult. The use of a pole or sling held by the teacher which an adult can hold for extra support can encourage 'feet off the bottom of the pool' and then movement across the pool. This enables the swimmer to feel the stimulation of water flowing over the skin which derives from movement.

Some learners who are obese or those who have little body awareness may have difficulty in regaining a standing position, particularly from a supine float or glide. They should either proceed to the side of the pool to rest or learn to rotate to a prone position then stand up.

A teacher should find out why adults have joined the class and what they hope to achieve, and then adapt the teaching to their particular needs. Try to give them a safe method of entry other than down the steps, and a way of climbing out from deep water. The ability to move safely out of their depth, to tread water and to scull are skills which may be needed should they wish to go on to learn sail boarding, canoeing or other water sports.

Fig 83   Supporting in a prone position to help the feel of a long body
and leg position.

Adult Non-Swimmers

Some adults joining non-swimmer classes want very quick results; they may come to learn to swim ready for a holiday planned for just a few months ahead; and they are usually highly motivated to achieve success. Others will be very slow to learn through a deep-seated fear of participation in any water activity.

The teacher must always teach in a way which gives the swimmer an understanding of safety as well as movement in water. Adults must be aware of their own capability and know their limitations,

particularly when swimming in open water.

The Persistent Non-Swimmer

This group is made up of those children and adults who have received instruction previously, even over an extended period, and yet have failed to swim. They require special attention if they are to succeed. Initially it is necessary to identify why they have so far failed to make progress.

Fear of the water or of the particular

swimming situation is usually the main cause in preventing someone learning even simple watermanship skills. The aim of the teacher must be to alleviate the fear, for if this is accomplished then water skills can usually be learned with ease. The way in which fear manifests itself will vary with each individual. Some people will make every effort to avoid attending swimming sessions; others may appear outwardly calm thus masking a high state of anxiety which is not appreciated by the teacher. Anxiety is an integral part of a learner swimmer's experiences, and can seriously impede the learning process. Some learners cannot absorb new information in a lesson because their attention is focused on their own internal struggle. This can lead to the learner refusing to carry out certain tasks because fear overrides any desire to achieve. Some may attempt the set task but movements will be awkward and uncoordinated through excessive muscle contraction.

The teacher must examine the factors which may be causing the anxiety or in-built fear of water or the swimming situation. These could include:

● A conditioned response from a previous unpleasant water experience. This may have been an accident, a single frightening experience, or may be persistent reaction to previous unsympathetic and unsuitable teaching.
● A response to water learned from parents who are non-swimmers and themselves have a fear of water activities.
● Environmental factors such as the feel, taste or temperature of the water, and a noisy, crowded building.
● Fear of failing, particularly in the eyes of a peer group.

● Expectations which create pressures to succeed. These expectations may be from ambitious parents, teachers with preconceived ideas, or even from the non-swimmers themselves.

The teacher has a significant role to play in helping to overcome fear. It may mean a complete change in approach in the teaching of swimming to try to counter-condition the acquired fear. To do this a teacher should examine carefully the previous 'swimming' experiences of the non-swimmer. It may help to discuss the problem with the parents if appropriate. The teacher should always discuss the problem with the adult or child so that they consciously address the difficulty and perhaps go some way towards eliminating fear by appreciating the cause. The expectations of the parent, the teacher and the learner should then be carefully analysed, and realistic goals set.

Once there has been some analysis of the problem the teacher should adapt teaching methods and programme lesson content to try to achieve success with the individual. Facilities should be as pleasant as possible, warm, quiet and colourful. Learning should be in a small group, with a competent swimmer in the water to give additional guidance. Regular daily lessons are preferable to spaced weekly attendance, because more continuous exposure to learning a task avoids wasting time on re-learning and reinforces good swimming habits.

The use of buoyancy aids, their type and number, must be carefully considered for each individual. The addition of music or toys when appropriate helps relaxation and creates a play-like atmosphere. Teaching should be through a watermanship programme (*see* chapter 3) with emphasis on balance, breathing, and free movement rather than on stroke production. Any targets set must be attainable, and the swimmer made aware of his or her successes. The learner must be given constant feedback and, when necessary, a change of practice to achieve the sub-skill or goal of the activity.

Lessons should be paced to allow learning to occur and to provide a satisfactory experience for the learner. The use of 'fun' activities encourages learning through involvement, and a partner system may be appropriate. Achievement can be recorded by the teacher and learner; this may include the use of a progressive award system.

Wetting the face is often feared by learners, so the teaching should be adapted to achieve movement with the face clear of the water until further confidence has been gained. Above all, the teacher must consider the needs of each individual. There can be a tendency to ignore the persistent non-swimmer rather than give the extra attention needed. Giving extra attention can, of course, be difficult in a school class situation.

Making the learning of water skills enjoyable, even to the initially frightened non-swimmer, and increasing the teacher's awareness of early problems, should help to remedy the difficulties of a persistent non-swimmer group.

Fig 84   Light hand support to give minimal help following a push and glide.

Fig 85   A helper avilable if needed as a swimmer attempts a back glide with a leg kick.

Adult Improver Groups

Whenever possible, adults should be encouraged to continue their swimming after the beginning stage for both safety and fitness. To continue to work in a group can be more challenging and gives greater learning opportunities. The teacher should now aim towards good performance in all strokes, dives, synchronised swimming skills, survival, life saving and water games. Adults enjoy learning a variety of skills and want to try all aspects of swimming. There will always be variations to the pace of participation and learning, and whilst the tasks set by the teacher may now be more restrictive in their interpretation the distance covered by each swimmer will vary and the teaching will still be very individual.

Improver class members appreciate the opportunity to test themselves by taking awards. Some become interested in the teaching of swimming and can become very useful members of a club or become helpers in a swimming club for people with disabilities.

Some members of improver groups continue to attend for the social contacts they make, and because they enjoy being part of a group that meets regularly. These classes can also act as water therapy for swimmers with disability.

The teacher should refer to chapter 7 for any special teaching methods required by these people.

The teacher should use a variety of strokes, including side-stroke, dog paddle and life-saving back-stroke as it may be easier for older swimmers to move with their limbs always underwater (*see* chapter 3).

Aqua-Fit Programmes

It is now accepted that exercise promotes the healthy function of various body systems and reduces the likelihood of heart disease. To these ends, water can be used as a gymnasium to develop a fitness programme. For the groups considered in this book, adults, the elderly and those with physical, mental, or sensory impairment a health-related fitness programme is essential. Water supports the body but it also offers resistance for exercise and this resistance can be varied. Whilst swimming exercises the body it does not place stress on the joints, as many other forms of exercise do. Both swimmers and non-swimmers can participate in an aqua-fit programme, the non-swimmers using buoyancy aids for support. Whatever programme is selected, in order to be beneficial it must fulfil certain criteria.

Criteria for an Aqua-Fit Programme

1 A warm-up period when the mind and body are gradually introduced to activity and the heart rate is gradually increased.

Fig 86 Adult aqua-fit group.

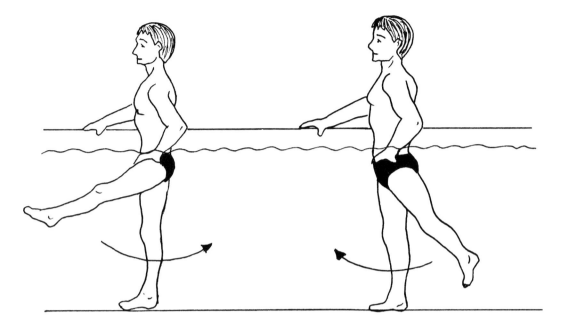

Fig 87   Forward and backward leg swings with support at the rail.

2   A period of activity which lasts for a minimum of 20 minutes; this will be gradually developed over a series of lessons.
3   Exercises which improve suppleness, strength and stamina.
4   Exercises which stretch the different parts of the body before subsequent vigorous activity.
5   A warming-down period at the end of the lesson consisting of milder exercise to help the body recover more quickly.

There should be a gradual increase in the intensity of the programme, which must be carefully monitored by or for each individual. It is essential that all participants understand the basic principles behind their own fitness programme. There should be regular participation in exercise at least three times a week and

where possible swimming should be one of several different types of exercise undertaken. For some people swimming will be their only form of exercise and in these cases the fitness aspect must be stressed, and in particular the necessity for regularity of participation. The programme presented should always readily encompass different swimming abilities.

Teaching Aqua-Fit

It is not the intention within this book to detail all the exercises and activities which may be used in an aqua-fit programme, only to outline the basic principles. A swimming teacher with a good understanding of exercises or dance can adapt material to suit work in a pool. Anyone wishing to teach aqua-fit must be

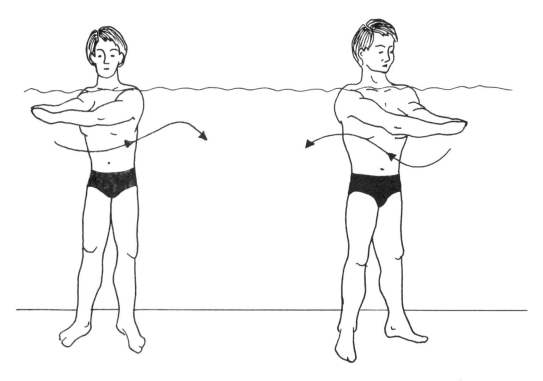

Fig 88   Arm exercise, standing with shoulders under the water to use water resistance.

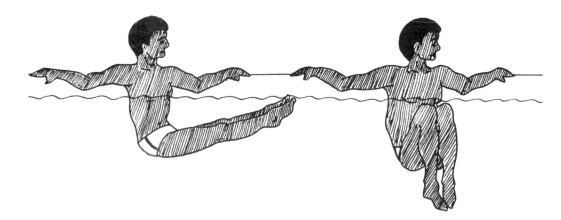

Fig 89   Exercise for trunk and legs taking the legs in different directions, both bent and straight.

a qualified swimming teacher and understand how exercise affects the body, particularly the cardiovascular and respiratory systems, and the reasons for selecting exercises to effect the suppleness or strength of different body parts.

Exercise in water should normally use the water to give resistance or support to the body, for otherwise the benefits of exercising in water are lost. Some exercises are easier to perform in the water because of the assistance given by the upthrust of the water, whereas some exercises can be made more difficult by pushing or pulling against the resistance of the water. Resistance can be increased by enlarging the surface area involved, such as holding a float in the hand or using a paddle or weight.

High rates of exercise can be achieved from aqua-fit when required. The programme should have various components including the exercise of specific body parts performed with or without music, movement in water, circuit training in water, water games, movement sequences to music, distance swimming and timed swims.

An increase in intensity can suit each individual by increasing resistance, increasing repetitions, increasing the pace and increasing the distance covered when moving in water. Teachers or individual swimmers themselves can

Fig 90   Treading water whilst keeping a ball in the air. An activity demanding strength and stamina.

devise an exercise programme which will improve suppleness, strength and stamina. This can be used as a basic programme repeated regularly and advanced through an increase in resistance, time or repetitions. An example of an exercise programme is given in Appendix 4.

Ante and Post-Natal Groups

Water is an excellent medium for exercising during pregnancy. The buoyancy of the water makes the body weightless and therefore freer to move. The support given to the body makes injury less likely during exercise. It provides valuable strengthening and flexibility work for the back, pelvic region, the chest and the legs, the body parts most likely to be affected by carrying additional weight and by the changing body shape.

Ideally, water exercise should be started as soon as possible in a pregnancy. This may take place in an aqua-fit class, or in a particular session for ante and post-natal exercises.

Post-natal exercises help muscles to regain their strength and the body generally to regain normal muscle tone. Water exercise helps with relaxation and general fitness, which are so essential both during and after pregnancy. All water exercises are valuable in retaining range of movement in the joints, but for ante and post-natal women there should be concentration on the spine, pelvis, abdomen and on breathing.

Breathing should be rhythmical whilst exercising or swimming, the swimmer concentrating on breathing out and blowing bubbles. Breathing out strongly

will automatically be followed by deep and strong inhalation, but care should be taken to avoid hyperventilation.

Some suggested exercises are given in Appendix 4; all of these can be used or adapted for use in ante and post-natal classes. With antenatal groups, as the pregnancy progresses less strain will be placed on the body by lifting a leg bent, rather than straight, by reducing the number of repetitions or the pace of action. In antenatal classes, the return to exercise should be easy and then gradually increase as muscle tone and fitness are developed. The adults themselves must be sensible and avoid excessive strain, and the women must have discussed their involvement in an exercise programme with their physician beforehand.

Pregnant women enjoy attending these classes, as they find the warm water relaxing and enjoy a freedom of movement which they tend to lose on land. The sessions can be combined with adult aqua-fit or with parent and baby groups. The women appreciate being one of a group of pregnant or post-pregnant women and enjoy the opportunity to socialise and chat. If it is possible to have a midwife present for some if not all of the classes, many questions can be answered. This involves, more officially, the health services in this valuable exercise therapy.

Swimming for Fitness

As has been said, swimming is widely recognised as one of the best methods of gaining or retaining a desirable level of fitness. There are many adults who are reasonably competent swimmers, and who can be encouraged to join a swim-fit group. Some of them may, as a result of the ageing process, illness or accident, have physical or sensory impairment. This need not handicap them when swimming. All can work on their own programmes using the stroke or method of propulsion most suited to their abilities. Nevertheless the teacher must not underestimate the ability of elderly swimmers and should always try to improve their technique as well as their stamina. Suppleness and strength may gradually be regained through swimming which will facilitate the performance of orthodox strokes, starts and turns.

As with the aqua-fit and ante and post-natal groups, the opportunity to swim several times a week proves enjoyable and becomes a regular way of life for these people. Masters swimming groups engaged in competitions incorporate all ages from 25 years to 80 years and over.

There are a variety of ways in which a teacher, coach or individual swimmer can plan and vary a swim-fit training programme. The aim will differ for each individual, from those swimming a set distance regularly to those wishing to train to swim competitively in a masters programme.

Suggested Tasks

(i)   Swim a set distance on each visit to the pool and record the accumulated total distance covered.
(ii)   Swim a predetermined distance aiming at a target time. Swimmers set their own pace, recording any progress made and then re-setting targets.
(iii)   Vary the strokes used and the distance covered on each stroke.
(iv)   Use part practices: legs only, arms only and then whole stroke.

(v)   Add one or two speed swims in a session: a length, two lengths or more, at a faster pace.

Guidelines for Swimmers and Teachers

Do not be over-ambitious when returning to swimming, but begin by swimming easily for 10 to 15 minutes using easy strokes and sculling for propulsion, and stop to rest when necessary, thus avoiding strain. Gradually increase the length of time for a continuous swim and increase the number of times for swimming each week, aiming for at least three sessions a week. Try to swim faster for a short distance, and set an interesting programme which can be repeated on each visit until it is easy. Then increase distance or speed, or vary the tasks.

A Sample Programme

1   Five minutes warm-up – easy, continuous swimming using a variety of strokes.
2   Swim 50 metres (55 yards) fairly hard. Rest for 45 seconds or 1 minute; repeat three times.
3   Swim continuously for 5 minutes.
4   Swim 50 metres (55 yards) hard. Rest for 1 minute, repeat once.
5   Swim continuously for 3 minutes.
6   Scull for 3 minutes.

The times and distances may be varied according to the target set by each individual, but most of the swimming should be fairly hard in an effort to raise the pulse rate. Keeping a log of what is achieved in a session acts as self-motivation. Where a teacher or coach is leading a group they must set targets which are achievable but which challenge the adults. An assessment of progress will encourage continued participation and this is important for all adults. Better swimmers may wish to join a swimming club which caters for masters swimming, and which give the opportunity for participation in competitive events.

Swimming in a Multi-Ethnic Society

Multi-ethnic education should permeate all aspects of sport, including swimming; teachers should make any necessary adjustments to involve the whole community in mainstream swimming. In any of the swimming groups considered in this book there are likely to be members of different ethnic groups all participating fully, with equal opportunities for swimming being offered. There are however certain cultural customs and religious beliefs which have an effect on involvement. None of the difficulties are insuperable and concessions have to be made to facilitate participation.

Muslim girls and women traditionally keep their bodies covered and have no contact with males who are not relatives. Single sex swimming sessions should be arranged and suitable light clothing worn. Special school pools can often give the privacy required to encourage certain cultural groups of women to join in swimming.

Language should not be a barrier where mime can be used or partners used to interpret the teacher's instructions. Adults from minority ethnic groups should be encouraged to train as swimming teachers themselves, and all teachers or club leaders must make every effort to gain a basic understanding and knowledge of the cultures of ethnic minorities and to be sensitive to their particular needs. Safety factors must always be observed. Where the wearing of religious symbols or artefacts is necessary, a means of covering them whilst swimming to prevent accidents can be devised.

Some groups will require considerable motivation to become involved in swimming. Discussions with parents, adult groups and community leaders may help to solve problems and indicate a flexibility of approach. The value of swimming and its safety aspects should be stressed when explaining to parents and community leaders the need for participation in this sport.

7 Teaching People with Disabilities

The selection of material to be used in swimming, and its adaptation, should relate to the special needs of the individual even when teaching groups of people with the same or similar disabilities. Assumptions about factors common to all of them should be avoided and should not be based solely on factors relating to their disability. Whilst in this chapter some emphasis is placed on the nature of an impairment and the associated movement problems, a teacher should always focus on the potential of pupils, on their ability and not their disability.

It is helpful to define terms, here using the definitions adopted by the World Health Organisation. Impairment is 'any loss or abnormality of psychological, physiological or anatomical structure or function'. Disability is 'any restriction or lack, resulting from an impairment of ability to perform an activity within the range considered normal for a human being'. Handicap is 'a disadvantage for a given individual, resulting from an impairment or disability, that limits or prevents the fulfilment of a role that is normal, depending on age, sex, social or cultural factors, for that individual'.

Individuals who are disabled because of impairments are limited in executing some skills. To illustrate this distinction, consider the case of a paraplegic confined to a wheelchair as the result of an accident. The impairment is the spinal lesion resulting in paralysis of the legs and lower parts of the body. The primary disability is in the loss of the ability to walk though there will be other manifestations of the impairment. Handicaps only arise when the individual reacts with the environment in some way. If swimming is the chosen activity the disability will create some problems when transferring from the wheelchair to the water. When swimming the handicap may be minimal, particularly if there is developed strength in the upper part of the body.

This chapter attempts only to outline some of the more common conditions and the ways in which an impairment may interfere with skill performance and adjustment to water. For each impairment particular safety factors and teaching methods are listed.

Learning Difficulties

The categorisation of children and adults with learning difficulties is to be avoided as all individuals vary considerably in their achievements. They do not conform to the descriptions of one category only, the ability range is very wide and children will always progress at different rates. In general children with learning difficulties may be described as slow developers, some very slow. The expectation of the teacher should not be influenced by the physical appearance of the child. The teacher should be aware that some children may have hidden physical disabilities. For instance, there tends to be a greater incidence of epilepsy among those who have suffered brain damage. Also, children with Down's syndrome may frequently have cardiac or respiratory problems.

Behavioural Problems

There are certain behavioural problems which could cause severe learning difficulties: self isolation and the desire to preserve routines; lack of self-help skills; unsocial and inappropriate behaviour; hysterical and unnecessary physical reactions; attention-seeking and imaginary physical symptoms; obsessions, particularly with inanimate objects; unpredictability; lack of verbal communication or echolalia (the meaningless repetition of speech); extreme problems with relationships; lack of a sense of fear; distractability, which is the inability to concentrate attention on any particular person or object in the environment; hyperactivity (excessive activity); and perseveration, which is the inability to change easily from one activity to another.

Perceptual- Motor Problems

Many pupils who experience problems with motor skills exhibit problems related to perception imagery and memory. Included are such characteristics as: awkwardness or clumsiness; problems of laterality or directionality (see Glossary); poorly developed body-awareness; poorly developed kinaesthetic awareness and fine motor skills; poor visual perception causing difficulty in determining the size, shape and texture of an object; and auditory perception problems where pupils may be able to hear clearly but cannot properly organise the words in sequence.

Teaching

Teachers of those with learning difficulties must establish clear safety routines. They should be constantly aware of safety, and of the following factors, which will help to provide a good learning situation. Teach on a one-to-one basis, and always establish eye-to-eye contact with the swimmer. The use of inanimate objects encourages a response, and personal space for movement should be allowed for the anti-tactile. Break down skills to sub-skills, and use positive reinforcement as a reward for success. Reinforce kinaesthetic awareness and use movement exploration and a multi-sensory approach to teaching. Positive reinforcement can be used to shape new skills, and verbal information should be presented slowly, carefully and in small phrases. Use group activities and games of a simple construction, and don't be afraid to adopt a firm attitude when required.

Swimming is a sport in which there are not too many perceptual components, and for pupils with learning difficulties it offers them the opportunity to participate without requiring complex perceptual judgements involving three-dimensional space. To travel in water individually does not require the same order of decisions as striking or catching a ball, for instance. Pupils are able to gain satisfaction from easily measurable attainment. Teachers must be aware, however, that the first exposure to water may be a frightening and difficult experience as it is a very unique and different environment. They must be very supportive and the environment must be acceptably stable without unnecessary distractions. It may take a long time for initial confidence to be gained. Patience and reinforcement of skills, constant motivation and feedback will be necessary to ensure any level of success with some pupils. It will be necessary to reappraise objectives constantly so as to avoid a feeling of failure, if the challenge is to be met successfully.

Sensory Disabilities

Blind and Visually Impaired

Conceptual and perceptual differences in blind pupils hinge on two interacting factors: whether the blindness is partial or total, and the age of onset of blindness. Children who are congenitally blind or who lose their sight early in life will have no concept of a swimming stroke and will be entirely dependent on their other senses to gain this information. Those with a visual impairment are usually very good pupils, because they concentrate and are likely to carry out the teacher's instructions implicitly.

Safety

Ensure that the immediate environment is safe; doors should not be left ajar and floors should be clear of small apparatus. An emergency procedure must be fully understood; in particular the supervisor must have easy access to auditory signals

for those who swim independently. Ensure that the names of all pupils are known before the class starts, because communication with indivuals who cannot see requires the use of names. The needs of those pupils with a visual impairment must also be known to other pool users.

Avoid using non-permanent orientation aids, such as a metronome or cassette recorder, as in the end this will detract from independence. When teaching children who are visually impaired, always ensure they are aware of their pool position if you leave them to swim independently. Encourage pupils to swim initially with head up and ears clear of the water so that they may orientate themselves. Swimming in the outside lanes is advantageous for the visually impaired as the swimmer is able to hear the movement of the water against the wall of the pool.

Teaching

Independence is to be encouraged at all times, and a teacher should watch carefully to ascertain the amount of help which may be needed. However, supervision should be constant. Some partially-sighted pupils may appear to have more sight than is the case; in fact, they may not be able to distinguish movement in demonstrations or to see across a pool. A teacher must be aware of this. Swimming can be successfully accomplished once the initial difficulties of orientation and skill learning are overcome.

When introducing those who have a visual impairment to the new environment of a swimming pool, at least one session may be needed for orientation purposes. This session should be conducted with a helper serving as a guide.

The pupil should take the arm of the helper and be allowed to feel any changes in floor or wall textures, the location of benches, lockers, showers and toilets, and the route to the pool, counting paces as a means of measuring distance. The helper should maintain a near-constant dialogue, describing the facilities, so enabling the subject to form a mental image of the facility. To introduce swimming skills, use is made of a multi-sensory approach with carefully planned progression, emphasising touch and hearing. A progression in teaching may take the following form:

1 Describe the skill on land.
2 Demonstrate the skill on land slowly, with pupils touching the demonstrator to enforce aural communication.
3 The pupils try the skill with manual correction from the teacher or sighted partner.
4 Repeat the demonstration in the water with the pupils again touching the demonstrator.
5 Individuals practise, with verbal correction and feedback from the teacher or sighted partner.

If a blind person is not making progress the teacher should appraise the teaching techniques being used. The blind person may be very timid until readjustment to the strange environment has taken place. The teacher must try not to rush the pupil as this may cause distress and muscle tension. After the initial adjustment and learning of basic swimming strokes and skills the blind swimmer can be completely independent in water and swim competitively or recreatively with ease and enjoyment in a mainstream situation.

Deaf and Hearing-Impaired

As with the visually handicapped, few hearing-impaired people suffer from total disability. With the assistance of a hearing aid those with partial hearing may have good speech, but as the hearing aid must be removed prior to swimming, there will be a need to adjust to a sudden loss of hearing. Speech and communication will be affected, but some may be able to lip-read or to use sign language.

Safety
A medical certificate is needed, indicating whether total immersion of the head in water is advisable. Emergency procedures must be clearly understood and pupils must learn to respond immediately to visual cues. All pupils should be taught to keep their eyes open, particularly under water. Children with hearing impairments may have problems with balance. The teacher should be aware of this when introducing such skills as tumbling, jumping and diving.

Teaching
The teacher will find that pupils will demonstrate a wide variation in their abilities to perceive language and musical sounds. A poor or inappropriate response to an instruction may stem from an inability to associate words with their meanings. Nevertheless, once communication problems have been overcome the hearing-impaired pupils can participate fully in a mainstream swimming programme. When teaching swimming skills, good eye contact should be maintained, the teacher should face the pupil and keep still, and normal speech should be used. The teacher should avoid speaking slowly or over-emphasising words

and appreciate that some pupils may have a limited understanding of words. Always check that instructions have been understood.

Stand clear of any glare or shadow which may make lip-reading difficult. The use of visual aids, posters, skill sheets, and schedule lesson plans on the poolside all enhance understanding and video can be used to improve the understanding of stroke performance. Use a multi-sensory approach, emphasising visual demonstrations. Ask the swimmer questions to help assess understanding. The use of a 'buddy', or 'partner' situation aids communication, the hearing partner providing visual signals as required.

For those swimmers who are not permitted to have water in their ears, a modified stroke with the head held out of the water should be taught. Work is at present being carried out on the development of ear plugs which will keep the ear free from water.

Physical Disabilities

Cerebral Palsy

This is a condition arising from damage to the motor areas of the brain before or during birth, or in the first few years of life. It is a broad term concerning a variety of non-progressive motor disfunctions and results in a wide range of disabilities and severity of disabilities, from minimal handicap to very severe.

Types of Cerebral Palsy

Spasticity
This type of cerebral palsy results in persistent and increased muscle tone. There will be tense and inaccurate voluntary movements, and movement is usually jerky and restricted. The person may have learning difficulties and speech disorders, and may startle easily.

Athetosis
There will be involuntary movements and purposeless motion resulting in writhing movements. These may be accompanied by hearing, visual or speech impairments.

Ataxia
Ataxia results in a lack of directional control and balance. Movements are slow and awkward, and there will be a 'drunken' type of gait. There is a reduced sense of balance, as a result of which ataxia sufferers fall frequently. There may be a speech impairment.

Rigidity
This type of cerebral palsy results in continuous muscle tension, and movement is very difficult. The person may have severe learning difficulties.

Tremor
Tremor results in uncontrolled, involuntary, rhythmic movements. The tremor is increased with voluntary movements.

Mixed
Mixed cerebral palsy involves more than one type, none of which is predominant. The person may have multiple handicaps.

Classification of Disabilities

Monoplegia	Only one limb.
Paraplegia	Only the legs.
Hemiplegia	Limbs on one side of the body.
Diplegia	Legs primarily, arms slightly.
Quadriplegia	All four limbs.
Triplegia (rare)	Three limbs are involved, usually the legs and one arm.

The wide variety and severity of resulting handicaps make it important for a teacher to have a profile of each individual indicating specific motor handicaps, problems with balance, learning and communication difficulties. The most important factor, as far as the teacher is concerned, is the potential for independent movement.

Safety

As the musculature concerned with swallowing and breathing is frequently affected, the swimmer may have shallow breathing, an inability to blow, a reduced ability to cough and difficulty in swallowing. The combination of these factors means that water entering the mouth cannot be prevented from entering the lungs. It is important therefore to try to avoid this happening whilst swimming. If water enters the lungs, the pupil should be removed from the water, placed in the prone position with the legs raised higher than the head and pummelled on the back to try to pump the water out. The pupil should then be placed in the sitting position with the helper kneeling behind. The arms of the helper are placed round the pupil and over the diaphragm, the helper giving a series of short jerks which may stimulate the cough reflex. If able to co-operate, the pupil should be asked to huff with each jerk. Following such an incident the pupil should be under medical supervision as severe chest infection may occur.

Teaching

Although there is a wide range of abilities and problems there are certain common factors for teaching swimming. Activities that cause excitement or are too highly arousing should be avoided. The pool environment should be structured to minimise excitable external stimuli such as sudden loud noises or sudden movements. Create a calm atmosphere and aim to induce relaxation in the water. The water should be warm, and an interesting programme developed. The use of gentle swaying movements and suitable musical accompaniment can also help with relaxation. Assess an individual's range of movement and adapt skills to enable the swimmer to accomplish tasks successfully, for example rotation or propulsion in the water. Breathing practices, breath holding, blowing out and bobbing can help speech problems through the emphasis on breath control. One-to-one teaching will be necessary, particularly in the early stages of water orientation. For some pupils one-to-one teaching will always be necessary.

As pupils with cerebral palsy tend to have poor body images and lack an awareness of their movement capabilities, teaching through movement exploration and simple games helps emphasise the use of body parts and the practising of body skills and movement patterns.

Some pupils may never achieve independent swimming skills. However, the opportunity for them to gain sensory stimulation and enhance movement abilities can be more important than actually swimming.

Parkinson's Disease

This is a progressive disease of older people where there is constant movement of the hands and feet. The limbs gradually become spastic, balance is affected, there is loss of sensation in the limbs, and poor circulation.

Teaching and care are similar to those for cerebral palsy. Swimming is considered a useful part of therapy if the adult can be motivated to participate regularly. There may be respiratory problems, making blowing and coughing difficult.

Spina Bifida/Paraplegia

Spina bifida is a congenital condition whereby there is a deformity of the spine causing damage to the nerves which communicate movement and feeling. This damage may be in the form of a complete lesion or may be only mild. In its severest form there will be complete loss of motor and sensory function below the lesion. The extent of the disability will therefore depend on the position of the lesion and its severity. The physical characteristics are that of paraplegia, a flaccid paralysis and wasting of the lower limbs and in most cases incontinence. In some cases of spina bifida, retention of information is poor and apparently bright conversation can hide what is sometimes a complete lack of understanding. Teaching may need to be adjusted to compensate.

Teaching

As there is no sense of feeling in total paraplegia, particular care must be taken to ensure that the lower limbs are not exposed to potentially dangerous situations such as abrasive floors or hot pipes. The dragging of limbs along the poolside or even the pool floor in very shallow water is likely to cause cuts and sores which, because of poor circulation, may take a long time to heal. Owing to the lack of muscle in the lower limbs, and often a higher distribution of fat, these people benefit from extreme buoyancy when in water. If using their arms to give propulsion, they find swimming an ideal activity. However, when supine the legs tend to float extremely high in the water and this can lead to problems with balance and difficulties in recovering to an upright position. Raising the head forward slightly will lower the body position in the water. In the prone position, the hips will be high but the legs will tend to hang low in the water, particularly when the head is raised in the breast-stroke. Conversely, when the head is lowered as in the front crawl stroke the legs will drift to the surface.

Hydrocephalus

There is a high likelihood (75 per cent) of those affected by spina bifida also suffering hydrocephalus. This is caused by an obstruction in the circulation of the cerebro-spinal fluid around the spinal cord and brain. The actual condition of hydrocephalus is an accummulation of this fluid in a part of the brain. As with other conditions, there will be variations in the severity of damage caused by fluid pressure on the brain cells. This problem is usually arrested by the insertion of a drainage valve behind the right ear, just below the surface of the skin. A person suffering from hydrocephalus can sometimes be recognised by the enlarged nature of the head. With young children the skull is still growing and will expand to accommodate the pressure. Providing the condition is detected sufficiently early, or is not too severe, the resulting brain damage can be minimal or even non-existent.

Teaching

The teacher must exercise particular care and be constantly aware of certain safety factors:

● Avoid knocks to the head.
● Avoid the head being held.
● Avoid swimming at depth.
● Avoid the wearing of tight swimming caps.
● Be aware of any changes in behaviour or headaches which might be caused by a fault in the brain drainage system.
● Beware of the heaviness of the head upsetting body balance and causing difficulties in regaining an upright position.

Poliomyelitis

This is a virus which damages the motor nerve cells in the spinal cord during an acute infection, so causing loss of control in those muscles supplied by the motor nerves. Today, immunisation has meant that the occurrence of this disease and resulting disability are rare. The degree of paralysis will depend upon the extent of the damage to the nerves themselves. Paralysis may not be permanent and frequently only a number of nerve cells may be affected; consequently only

certain muscles will be paralysed. Disability can range from loss of movement in one finger through to quadriplegia. It should be noted that damage to motor nerve cells means loss of muscular control, but not necessarily loss of sensory input.

Teaching

Where the disability has been present for some time the body will have made appropriate adaptations to compensate for loss of specific muscle power. Teaching should aim to develop compensatory muscle power and movement. Always aim for maximum independence, adapting stroke styles and using residual muscle power. Adaptation of balance may be necessary.

Multiple Sclerosis

The cause of this particularly unpredictable disease is unknown. The damage caused by the disease, an eventual disintegration of the nerve fibres, is randomly distributed throughout the central nervous system so that there is considerable variation in its pattern and progress. For example, with some people the attack is acute, it develops rapidly and there is a quick onset of severe disability. Others may live for a normal life span. Remission periods are very common in this disease. Secondary complications may include: incontinence, particularly urinary; spasticity in lower limbs; impaired vision, particularly unilateral; obesity; and brain malformations, which may leave difficulties with memory and speech.

Teaching

Problems arise when the pupil is exposed to stress and fatigue; this is often not apparent until some time after the activity is finished. Problematic situations which might invoke stress, or long periods of activity which might cause fatigue should be avoided. Periods of 10 to 20 minutes of exercise are quite adequate. As much as possible should be taught during the swimmer's 'good' phases, so that confidence and water safety are already present when the subject is feeling less able. Emotional reactions to the disability may have a strong influence on the progress of the disease and so a positive approach and frequent success and encouragement are of particular benefit. The teacher must take account of any secondary complications and make any necessary adaptations in teaching method or content. Those who have already been swimmers will need help with balance and the adaptation of known techniques.

Strokes

A stroke is a layman's term for a haemorrhage, or interruption of the blood supply to the brain (i.e. a clot). A lack of blood supply, even momentary, results in a lack of oxygen supply which causes a degeneration of the brain cells. Initially there may be total paralysis of one side of the body (including the face) and this is of the spastic type. However, in most cases, physical recovery can be quite considerable. Such recovery of muscle control is usually more immediate in the leg, followed by a slower and less complete recovery in the arm. One of the biggest problems is that of communication. Although intellect is not impaired, difficulties in verbal communication can be major.

Teaching

The teacher should aim to help physical rehabilitation, improving leg movements and helping to relax any spasticity in the arm. To overcome psychological difficulties associated with the stroke, easily attainable goals should be presented, and safety skills may need to be re-introduced, particularly where balance is a problem. When teaching, understand that the difficulties in communication may be caused by a lack of muscular control of speech mechanisms causing slurring; hearing and comprehension are not impaired. It can be very hurtful to the swimmer to raise the voice, or use exaggerated or slow speech.

Muscular Dystrophy

This term refers to a group of related muscle diseases that are progressively incapacitating because the muscles gradually weaken and degenerate. Muscular dystrophy is hereditary and largely evident in boys.

Duchenne is the most prevalent type of muscular dystrophy and its effects are the most severe and progressive. The symptoms appear usually before the child is five years old, the early signs being difficulty in running, standing up and climbing up stairs. There is a tendency to fall, and regaining the feel is accomplished awkwardly. The disease progresses in stages from a mild waddling gait to a reliance on a wheelchair for ambulation; the ability to move the wheelchair independently will also decrease. Deformities are similarly progressive, with muscular contractions and skeletal distortion. Physical difficulties may be complicated by a tendency towards obesity.

Teaching

Respiratory failure is one of the major problems amongst those suffering from muscular dystrophy, so particular care should be taken to avoid chilling and an emphasis placed on activities encouraging breath control. As the disability progresses, muscular weakness and fatigue become common so long periods of strenuous exercise should be avoided. As the muscles of the back weaken, head control may be a problem and the necessary precautions should be taken, particularly when the swimmer is in the prone position. Much can be done by helping to maintain muscle strength, and in fact the only way of limiting muscular weakness is through regular exercise.

Some attempt should be made to prevent or at least deter secondary physical complications, such as obesity and muscle contractures, which lead to joint deformities, and although stretching exercises cannot cure, they certainly help. A positive approach is essential, whereby the teacher selects goals that the pupils will be able to attain.

Whilst the children are young they should be encouraged to live a full life, developing hobbies and making friends. Involving them in after school activities rather than allowing them to be inactive at home is good preparation for later life. Introducing them to swimming as early as possible gives the opportunity for a variety of water skills to be learned. At a later stage swimming may be the only physical activity that can be undertaken.

Arthritis

Arthritis is a joint condition characterised by inflammation, pain and swelling. The two general types of arthritis are osteo-arthritis, the degenerative type, and rheumatoid arthritis, the actual disease. The juvenile form of this disease is called Still's disease. Exercise is considered an essential part of the treatment for arthritis, and the affected joints should be moved through the greatest range of motion possible.

Osteo-Arthritis

Osteo-arthritis is the result of wear and tear in joints resulting in varying disabilities and pain which increase with age. It occurs primarily in the weight-bearing joints, and some people are more susceptible to this joint degeneration than others. Sporting activities such as jogging and those activities which put pressure on weight-bearing joints may for certain people increase the likelihood of contracting arthritis. Weakened muscles occur as a secondary complication.

Teaching

Cold conditions should be avoided; warm water can help movement in the joints. Many people with arthritis are more comfortable in the water, where weight bearing is removed, than on land. To help prevent a worsening of the condition, movement of the affected joints should be encouraged, and this should also help to maintain muscle strength. The teacher should plan an aqua-fit programme which incorporates movements for suppleness, strength and stamina to suit each individual. A preferred style of movement for the elderly arthritic may be sculling in a back layout position with a gentle alternating kick in the vertical plane.

Rheumatoid Arthritis

This is an inflammatory disease which can affect any joint in the body. It principally affects the fluid which lines and lubricates the joints. Swelling, pain and deformities result, and there is progressive worsening. Rheumatoid arthritis begins in youth, but affects different people with different degrees of severity. Swimming may be the most effective form of activity as it avoids weight bearing on joints which may be inflamed.

Teaching

Basically the teaching is the same as for osteo-arthritis, although joint and limb deformities can be much more dramatic in rheumatoid arthritis (particularly in Still's disease). Thought must be given to the choice of stroke and to body balance in the water, and great care in handling should be taken.

Congenital Deformities and Amputees

In the case of a congenital absence of one or more limbs, adaptations to balance are likely to create less problems as the body shape will feel 'normal', habitual adjustments having been made since birth. When a person has lost a limb due to an accident or illness, the major problem will be mental and physical adjustment.

Teaching a Recent Amputee

Privacy for changing may be desirable, and where an artificial leg is worn (prosthesis) changing facilities near to the poolside eases access to the pool. In order to overcome any psychological problems, early activities should be orientated toward frequent success. Balance and buoyancy need to be stressed, experimenting with the use of head, arm and leg movements to adjust positions in the water. Buoyancy aids may assist in gaining a balanced position and enable the swimmer to concentrate on swimming movements and rehabilitation of muscles.

Spinal Curvature

The causes of distortions of the vertebrae are numerous: unequal weakening of muscles, muscular dystrophy, poliomyelitis, spina bifida, bone deformities or bad posture. There are three spinal curvatures:

(i) Scoliosis – lateral curvature.
(ii) Lordosis – forward curvature.
(iii) Kyphosis – backward curvature.

Once there is a weakness in the spine and an asymmetry, the curvature can be progressive unless it is arrested by wearing a support, by strengthening the surrounding muscles or by surgery.

Teaching

The teacher should work to keep the cardio-vascular functioning of the body efficient, to strengthen muscles (particularly those around the trunk), and to maintain good posture and body symmetry.

Brittle Bones

This is caused by a congenital malformation of the bone structure, causing the subject to be exceptionally prone to fractures. As with all disabilities, there are degrees of severity. Where there are repeated fractures of different limbs, associated deformities arise and these may affect the body's balance and efficiency.

Teaching

Great care must be taken in the handling of pupils, particularly when assisting them in and out of the pool. Like all children they will enjoy playing water games but involvement in boisterous activity can be dangerous. If swimming on the back is taught the swimmer must be warned not to bump into the poolside. They should be encouraged to keep their eyes open at all times from the first introduction to the water.

With children who are more severely affected, very basic movement skills will need to be taught in the water as they will have had little opportunity for movement on land. Group activities should be encouraged as socialisation may be unfamiliar. Swimming is an ideal activity for these pupils, as the water is a protective environment, and strengthening the muscles through physical activity increases the protection of the bone. Teachers should therefore endeavour to give the swimmer full involvement within the bounds of safety.

Legge-Perthes Disease

This is a deformity of the hip joint, where the head of the femur is malformed. This disability, found in young children, is reversible; the bone generally repairs itself by laying down new bone. The growth centre is protected and the child wears a brace.

Teaching

There should be no weight bearing, but once supported by the water a full range of movements should be encouraged to help muscle strength.

Arthrogryposis

Arthrogryposis is a disease causing stiffness of the affected joints. Although weight bearing is possible, movement is naturally limited by tightness in the joints. As a result, muscles are usually wasted and the subject takes on the appearance of being very thin with deformed joints. The following physical effects of the disability may be present: shoulders turned in; elbows straightened; forearms turned palm down; wrists flexed inwards; fingers circled into the palms; hips flexed and turned out; knees either bent or straight; feet turned in and down; scoliosis of the spine; small limbs; large joints; and loss of motion.

Teaching

The main aim is to develop muscle power and flexibility within the limitations of the disability. Stroke adaptations may have to be made to overcome the effects of joint stiffness.

Invisible Disabilities

Epilepsy

To have epilepsy is to manifest a tendency to recurrent fits or seizures. An epileptic fit is caused by a sudden abnormal discharge of energy in the brain cells. The effects can range from major convulsions, with or without loss of consciousness, to minor absences of awareness or abnormal behaviour patterns. A person with epilepsy may have more than one type of fit. The following are the most common:

Absence (Petit-Mal)

This often goes unnoticed and is physically obvious only as a day-dream or momentary stare. It lasts for a few seconds, then the subject will return to normal activity. The teacher should be understanding, note that it has occurred and repeat any instructions or teaching points that may have been missed.

Tonic Clonic (Grand-Mal)

The subject may experience an aura before the fit. This is a good indication of the onset of a fit. The sequence may be staring, stiffening of the body and a cry followed by a fall and convulsions of the body. The subject may salivate. If the saliva is blood-flecked it indicates the tongue or cheek has been bitten. The fit may last five minutes at the most. The subject will then recover consciousness and feel dazed and confused for a period of several minutes to an hour. They are usually tired and may have a headache.

Procedure during a grand-mal:

1 Try to protect the head with hands, a cushion or clothing.
2 Turn the head to one side to avoid the tongue obstructing breathing.
3 Move any hard or sharp objects away.
4 Loosen clothing around the neck.
5 Stay with the subject and observe activities. *Do not* force anything into the mouth, restrain convulsive movements, lift or move the subject.

After a grand-mal, turn the subject into a recovery position to allow saliva to drain out of the mouth and facilitate breathing. Do not give a drink until the person is fully awake; call a doctor or ambulance unless one fit follows straight on from another (in which case stay with the person), or alternative instructions apply to a particular subject.

Complex

This originates in one part of the brain, and the results are variable. The subject may appear confused, with an involuntary twitching movement, plucking at clothes, and smacking of the lips. The subject appears conscious but may not respond. The fit may be quite long, leaving the subject confused. The procedure during a fit should be as follows: be understanding; remove harmful objects; talk reassuringly; do not try to restrain the movements.

In swimming, careful supervision is necessary. There should be close one-to-one supervision either from the poolside or in the water. Pool staff should always be informed if someone with epilepsy is intending to swim. The lifeguard must understand the procedures should a swimmer have a fit in the water:

1 The water provides a protective environment.
2 Keep the subject clear of the poolside.
3 Support the head to keep the face clear of the water.
4 When the fit is over, the subject should be helped from the water and allowed to rest in a warm place.

Provided the necessary safety measures are taken, those who have epilepsy should be encouraged to swim.

Diabetes

Diabetes is a metabolic disorder caused by a malfunctioning of the pancreas. It may be inherited and there are two variations. The milder form is that which materialises in later life, when a carefully controlled diet along with the taking of pills can control the condition. The more severe form is that which usually affects young people when the balance of blood sugar is maintained by injecting insulin.

Sufficient insulin has to be infiltrated into the blood stream to allow cells to utilise glucose from food for energy. Too much insulin can be harmful and the sugar level will fall too low. If there is insufficient blood sugar available to supply the brain cells with energy, then a reaction to excessive insulin, hypoglycaemia, takes place in the body. If untreated, this may lead to a diabetic coma. An insulin reaction takes place very quickly, unlike the less common problems with treated diabetes, namely a recurrence of the initial condition, or where there is a shortage of insulin (hyperglycaemia).

Control of diabetes is achieved by maintaining a balance between diet, insulin and exercise. Exercise is useful in the treatment of diabetes as it stimulates the action of the insulin by lowering the blood sugar, through the use of sugar in the muscles. Additional food should be taken before severe exercise to prevent hypoglycaemia. Hypoglycaemia and hyperglycaemia are quite distinct and they can be recognised from the following symptoms:

Too much insulin (insulin reaction/hypoglycaemia)
The onset symptoms are: unusual behaviour; rapid onset (minutes); headache; nausea; vomiting; palpitations; tremulousness; irritability. Skin will be cold and moist, breathing shallow or normal, and a urine test will show no sugar, because the blood contains too much insulin. The treatment is sugar.

Too little insulin (hyperglycaemia/ketoacidosis)
The onset symptoms are: gradual onset (hours or days); tiredness; increased output of urine; desire to drink; increased appetite but loss of weight. Skin will be warm and dry, breathing deep, and a urine test will show too much glucose and acetone because there is no insulin to convert these to energy. The treatment is insulin.

Regular exercise is as important as a regular intake of food and insulin. If participation in a prolonged activity is undertaken, a snack should be eaten every half hour. The teacher should encourage normal participation in swimming.

Haemophilia

This is a blood disorder resulting in the inability of the blood to coagulate. When the person with haemophilia experiences a wound, either internally or on the body's surface, bleeding is prolonged. Individuals with haemophilia should take part in regular exercise, and swimming is highly recommended as there is little risk of injury.

Teaching

Pupils should be taught to look carefully where they are going, take care when swimming on the back and avoid participation in very boisterous games or diving.

Cystic Fibrosis

This is a hereditary disease in children, where there is an abnormal secretion of mucus from glands of the body, primarily the pancreas. If the pancreatic glands become blocked and the enzymes it produces fail to reach the digestive organs, the food is not properly broken down. With poor digestion there is weight loss through malnutrition. There is also an extra secretion of salt from the sweat glands, which can become a problem in hot weather or after strenuous exercise. An accumulation of excessive mucus in the lungs can lead to infection of the bronchial tubes, hyper-inflation of the lungs and lung collapse. There is a particular susceptibility to pneumonia, bronchitis and other such respiratory infections. Keeping the lungs clear to avoid infections is a problem, and postural drainage is the main means of preventing this.

Teaching

Physical activity helps to clear the lungs and children should be encouraged to cough. A bowl and tissues should be kept on the poolside to collect mucus. Severe chilling should be avoided.

Asthma

Asthma causes spasmodic contractions of the bronchi, leading to wheezing, panting and severe breathing difficulties. Exercise Induced Asthma (EIA), as the title suggests, is the name given to an attack which occurs through exercise, and is common amongst most asthma sufferers. This condition is often very much misunderstood and has inherited many unnecessary fears. People who suffer from asthma find that air cools and dries the airways, thus causing breathing difficulties. Lack of fitness means more air has to be inhaled and the condition is therefore aggravated. Running activities may be more likely to trigger bronchospasm; because of the warm, damp atmosphere swimming may be the best activity for improving the overall condition of the asthma sufferer. Regular exercise should be continued throughout life. If EIA occurs during an activity it may be reversed by the advised medication. There is some evidence that keeping the pulse rate below 160 may help to avoid EIA.

Teaching

A teacher's aim must ultimately be to enable an asthmatic pupil to participate at the level of, and alongside, peers without asthma. The teacher should follow a normal teaching programme, but also records should be kept of fitness levels and progressions. Time before the start of the lesson may be required for medication or preliminary exercises. A warm-up period at the start of the lesson is important for asthma sufferers. The lesson should include short periods of activity followed by rest periods. The intensity and length of activities should be increased gradually. Difficulties with breathing or activities which cause breathlessness should be noted carefully. Blowing activities, encouraging forced expiration, should be included.

8 Forming a Club for Swimmers with Disabilities

Early Planning

Forming any sort of club, sporting or social, calls for much careful forethought. Preliminary investigations must be made into the potential and viability of the project, particularly when the club in question is that of a swimming club for persons with special needs.

There must, from the start, be a sureness and integrity of aims and objectives, allied to a pertinacity of purpose on the part of the planners. Every effort should be made to ensure the club's success, as failure on the club's part may be seen by those involved as a reinforcement of society's tendency to want to cut off the disabled person from the fun and enjoyment of living.

There is increasing awareness of the particular advantages offered by swimming to those with special needs who wish to participate in sporting activity. Swimming gives a unique opportunity for the disabled swimmer, in some instances, to achieve parity in performance with that of the swimmer of unimpaired abilities. It also provides, to a greater extent than any other sport, a meaningful opportunity for the integration of the disabled swimmer and the able-bodied helper, allowing a sense of achievement and satisfaction to both.

From the beginning, the club should be seen as belonging to the members, their active participation in the running of the club to be sought whenever possible. In this way the preservation of the essential dignity of the member will be safeguarded, a matter sometimes overlooked by able-bodied club officials overzealous in their efforts to 'do good'.

With the aims and objectives of the project clearly defined in their minds, and integrity of approach intact, the organisers can proceed with the preliminary groundwork, which will take a matter of months rather than weeks.

Need and demand having been established, and the type of club determined (and here let it be said that the most successful, and happiest, appear invariably to be those that embrace every kind of disability and handicap), the possibility of encountering a local duplication or overlapping of effort should be examined. Where there is found to be an overlap, it need not detract from the project since there will always be a hidden demand not catered for by existing facilities. However, facilities already in existence will offer new clubs the opportunity to learn from their experiences. If there happens to be a good local able-bodied swimming club it too might be willing to co-operate in the formation of a club for disabled swimmers, as an offshoot of the main club. There are now a number of such arrangements throughout the country, operating to the mutual benefit of both groups, often providing previously unforeseen career possibilities for enthusiastic helpers.

First Steps

The first priority is finding a suitable venue. This should not be hurried, as a wrong move in this respect could have serious consequences for the fortunes of the club. The ideal venue, that is, one providing the special facilities and layout the swimmer might require, is rarely if ever to be found. Indeed, it is only occasionally that simply adequate facilities are available. Toilets and showers approached by steps and too narrow entrances abound, as do pools completely devoid of handrails. It will, therefore, almost invariably be necessary to consider facilities that fall short of the ideal. Once the club is established, of course, there is quite often the possibility of persuading a caring local authority or pool owner to do something about certain discrepancies in one of their pools, particularly when it is tactfully pointed out to them that it is their statutory obligation to do so.

The next step is that of attracting local interest, for ultimate success will depend almost entirely upon the support and co-operation of several different bodies within the community. This can best be achieved by arranging an appointment with the local authority director of recreation and leisure, with the chairman of the subcommittee in attendance if possible. This meeting can be crucial to

the success of the club, and the organisers must be clear and purposeful in explaining their intentions. It is worth bearing in mind that 'sport and leisure' are becoming big business, and that you are asking the local authority to set aside financial considerations in favour of a degree of altruism. That such altruism does exist is borne out by the fact that not infrequently one hears of a club fortunate enough to obtain their session 'free of charge', a tremendous financial boon for the newly established club. At this meeting, all of the other names and addresses of necessary contacts can be obtained, as well as a proper introduction to the pool management. A meeting with the pool management should take place as soon as possible thereafter.

The vast majority of pool managements will wish to co-operate as much as possible within the limitations of available staff and session time, and at this stage such important matters as availability of qualified supervision and the preferred water temperature should be raised. By this time the organisers will have a fairly good idea of the most convenient time for the session, based upon the requirements of their potential members. Of course, availability will in the end dictate the results. An agreement on water temperature is very important as it will strongly influence the reaction of members in the initial stages. Raising water temperature is a matter that pool managements find it difficult to give way upon, because of the disproportionate costs involved. You should, however, be insistent, as water temperature is vital to the comfort of some disabled swimmers, both the elderly and those with circulatory and muscular problems, for whom chilly water can be dangerous. Cool water can also have very serious consequences for the epileptic swimmer. A temperature range of 82–86°F (28–30°C) is, therefore, to be recommended, preferably the upper end of this range.

An appointment with the director of the local social services is also to be recommended in the early stages. This person's council will hopefully be forthcoming on a generous scale, and advice can also be obtained on the possible pitfalls to avoid, as well as suggesting other people to approach for help once the club has been formed. The questions of transport, escorts to and from the pool, and help in the changing rooms, are always problematic, yet equally as important as the more obvious help required on the poolside and in the water. The social services, who will have wide local knowledge, can offer invaluable advice on such matters.

Inaugural Meetings

The next consideration should be an inaugural meeting. This should be arranged with care and attention to detail. The following are simply guidelines to be followed from the inaugural meeting until the establishment of the club. These notes are comprehensive but need not necessarily be taken as imperative to success. They should be pruned and tailored to suit circumstances. Swimming clubs for the disabled are often formed from small beginnings, by the parents, relatives or friends of the disabled person whose sole qualifications are determination and perseverance in their objectives. Frequently such small plants blossom best, and mistakes made early within a small club environment (and

there will be mistakes), are easier to correct. However, the ideal criteria, which these notes offer, are a useful guide.

People to Invite to the Inaugural Meeting

Sports centre manager and/or bath manager and staff.
Chairman of recreation and leisure sub-committee.
Recreation and leisure officer for the district.
Director of social services for the area.
Physical education officer for the area.
Representative of local colleges.
Social Services: Senior occupational therapists for the area. Social workers and home visitors for the area. Community services officer for the area.
Medical: General practitioners practising within the area. Doctors involved in rehabilitation. Physiotherapists at local hospitals. Remedial gymnasts. Nurses from local hospitals.
Chairman and secretary, coaches and teachers of the local able-bodied swimming club.
Chairman and secretary, coaches and teachers of the local Royal Life Saving Society club.
Chairman and secretary of the local disabled societies: Gateway clubs, blind, deaf, muscular dystrophy, multiple sclerosis, MENCAP, police, spina-bifida organisations, and the local PHAB Club.
A local Sports Council representative.
Headmasters/mistresses of local special schools.
Managers of local adult training centres.
Known interested disabled sportsmen and women, and other known interested disabled people.

Senior representatives of the British Red Cross and the St. John's Ambulance.
Local clubs: Lions, Rotary, Round Table, Inner Circle, Inner Wheel, Soroptimists, Scouts, Guides and the various Cadet bodies.
Representatives from the Amateur Swimming Association, British Sports Association for the Disabled (1987), National Association of Swimming Clubs for the Handicapped and the Association of Swimming Therapy.
Anyone else of known interest.

Preparation for Inaugural Meeting

The subject of a suitable hall for this meeting may well have been broached at the earlier meeting with the director of recreation and leisure, as quite often the local sports centre will have such a place available. If not, the local council might be encouraged to provide such a meeting place in the town hall or other suitable hall. Local schools can also be amenable in this respect. A brief synopsis of the reasons for the meeting and an agenda should then be mailed to those thought of as being interested. This, ideally, should be done three or four weeks before the meeting, and provision for the costs involved must be taken into consideration in the early stages of planning.

It has been found wise to avoid raising expectations and arousing enthusiasm amongst the disabled people in the district by inviting their general participation at this early stage, and it is better, therefore, to limit invitations to disabled people to those known to be interested in helping.

The success or failure of the projected club could well depend upon the effectiveness of its presentation at this meeting, and the efficiency with which the meeting is run might well go far towards convincing those attending of the merits of the cause. A good chairman is, therefore, essential, and if the organiser is not to act in this capacity, a well-briefed and able substitute must be arranged. The following checklist may assist:

1 Ensure and confirm that the details of the booking of the hall, time and date are correct.
2 Mail out the notice and agenda three to four weeks in advance.
3 Ensure the chairman and any other speakers are well briefed with all of the necessary facts and background to the project.
4 Ensure the arrangements for suitable refreshments have been made for the end of the meeting. This encourages free discussion and stimulates interest.
5 If audio-visual aids are to be introduced at some stage ensure that all the necessary equipment has been booked and that any person assisting with it has all the details.
6 Ensure there will be good, well-placed advertisements of the meeting, through the various media, posters in suitable places, such as public libraries, schools and colleges. The local council may well assist in this direction.
7 Ensure the seating arrangements are adequate and, where people with disability are to be accommodated, that the seating is suitably comfortable.

The Meeting

The organiser and his associates should arrive early to welcome people upon arrival, checking the names of invited guests against a prepared list. Hand round a register for all present to record their names and organisation. The tone of all the speakers should be enthusiastic; a disabled sportsman or woman of national or international reputation will provide just the right impact to fix attention.

The Chairman of the meeting will ask for volunteers to come forward from the audience to help on a committee to start the club; normally around a dozen will be adequate. The committee should consist of both able-bodied and disabled people. It is helpful, but not absolutely necessary, to have on the committee a doctor to act as medical adviser, and, if possible, one or two physiotherapists and two or three swimming coaches/teachers. One or two businessmen with town contacts can also be an asset to a committee such as this, as well as a representative from the Rotary, Round Table or the Lions. It should be made quite clear that previous committee experience is not necessary, but that each committee member must be prepared for real involvement.

A committee chairman, secretary or treasurer need not be nominated at this stage as this is better done at the first meeting of the committee after some careful consideration has been given to the matter. Before the meeting closes it is essential to obtain the names, addresses and telephone numbers of all the people elected to serve on the committee, and to arrange a date, time and place for the next meeting, the first of the committee as such.

First Committee Meeting

A chairman will be required to initiate the proceedings until the election of the committee chairman, and in this respect the organiser should ensure that a suitable person is ready to undertake this role at the first meeting. Invitations should be sent to all members of the committee, stating the date, time and place for the meeting. The agenda should also be included.

The committee structure should resemble that of Fig 91.

The first committee meeting should deal with a wide range of matters. Club identity and catchment area must be established, along with eligibility for, and

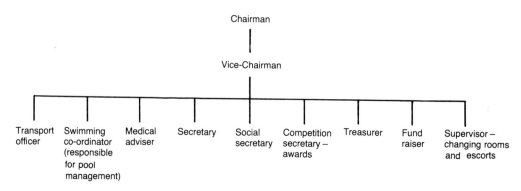

Fig 91   The structure of the swimming club committee.

types of, membership (honorary, associate, full). Club structure, and the pool and club management must be defined. What facilities will be available must be considered, and a constitution drawn up. The constitution must include the following:

Name (of the club).
Objectives (of the club).
Membership (number, eligibility).
Membership fees (how much, when collected).
Committee (structure, list of members).
Finance (raising and allocation).
Appointment of trustees, if thought necessary.
Annual General Meeting.
Dissolution (when and how).

The opening of a bank account for the committee's finances must be decided upon, and fund raising must be discussed. It should be noted that excellent insurance cover is obtainable through one or two existing associations directly concerned with swimming for the disabled, and the matter must be fully discussed. Transport must be arranged, and it must be decided how the club will go about contacting the disabled people it thinks will be interested. A president may be elected, and the usual committee procedures of 'any other business' and the arrangement of date and place of next meeting must be run through.

Duties of Club Officials

Club Management

The duties of the chairman, vice-chairman, secretary, treasurer, social secretary and fund raiser are essentially the same for any sports club.

Medical Adviser

Whilst it is desirable to have sound professional medical advice upon matters relating to disabilities, it is not vital to the formation of a club for disabled swimmers that there is a general medical practitioner on the committee. Once the type of club has been determined, the question of eligibility must be governed by the sound common sense and experience that will be on the committee by way of physiotherapists, paramedical helpers and the like. A certificate signed by the intending member's general practitioner should prevent an error of judgement, and close supervision and scrutiny by the swimming co-ordinator and his/her team in the first few weeks should eliminate any possible unforeseen dangers in this respect.

Transport Officer

A transport officer needs to be appointed by the committee at the earliest possible stage to allow time to make contact with social services, local clubs for the disabled, and, most importantly, possible helpers, such as the Lions, Rotary, local factories, colleges and special schools. This should result in a large list of voluntary people who are prepared to assist using their private transport. Transportation should only be arranged for the swimming members who are really in need of it. If one of the committee members with disability has a private telephone and is willing to undertake this duty, he or she should be encouraged to do so.

Swimming Co-ordinator

The swimming co-ordinators will be the people with overall responsibility for all activities both in the pool and on the poolside. Briefly, the roles and responsibilities of this position are as follows:

(i) Responsibility for all activities and safety in the pool and on poolside.
(ii) The overall activity programme, planning and organisation.
(iii) The recruitment of swimming, diving and life-saving teachers or coaches.
(iv) The recruitment of paramedical helpers: physiotherapist, remedial gymnast, nurses. Qualified swimming teachers who hold the Teacher's Certificate for Swimming for the Disabled, together with a physiotherapist and remedial gymnast as assistants make an excellent team.
(v) The recruitment of life-savers, instructors and poolside helpers.
(vi) Supervising the training of all recruited personnel, motivating them to improve their qualifications, and arranging time for the preliminary training of all new helpers. This latter is essential to the success of the programme and initially, until such time as it can be delegated to other instructors, could involve considerable personal involvement.

Training Programme for Helpers

The swimming co-ordinator will arrange for regular training sessions for the helpers, to include handling the disabled generally, assisting them to and from the pool, and the principles of balance and buoyancy as it affects the disabled learner swimmer. This training should also include understanding the nature of the common disabilities and the rudimentary application of life-saving techniques.

Supervisor-Escort/Changing and Dressing

This responsibility is so often overlooked that special mention should be made of the importance of this role in any club. If this task is performed efficiently it will relieve the swimming co-ordinator of much time-consuming preoccupation with the welfare of the members before they arrive. Most importantly, it will go far to preserve the dignity of the members who often, by the very nature of their disability, may feel extremely vulnerable initially and not at all confident in their ability to appear so exposed as swimming would seem to demand.

From the moment the members leave the transport an escort should be available to see them safely to the changing rooms. Here they should be helped quickly, quietly and carefully to prepare themselves for the pool. Care must be taken at all times to avoid bruising and abrasions to limbs, and encouragement given at this stage will provide the early confidence needed for the assimilation of water skills later. Additional care is required in escorting from the pool to the changing rooms, for the swimmers will be tired, and sometimes chilled. Efficiency in drying and dressing is essential, and the recruitment of the right helpers to achieve this is important. It is often found that young people have much aptitude for such assistance, and every encouragement should be given to them where help is offered.

Administration

Apart from application forms and medical certificates, the co-ordinator will determine what sort of records are kept. The following is a suggested list:

- Records of attendance by members and helpers.
- Records of each member.
- Records of each instructor/helper.
- Progress reports on each swimmer.

Matters for the newsletter and notice board, and application forms for galas should be forwarded to the club secretary or the competition secretary.

Safety and Equipment

Reference should be made to the chapters on facilities, safety and hygiene, and on teaching methods. All teachers and helpers must be fully aware of emergency drill procedures and constantly alert to the safety of the club members.

Appendix 1

Lesson Plans

Teacher's name ....

Time available for lesson ....   Time available for changing ....
Organisation details for changing room   ....
Individual needs in handling ....
Relevant details of facilities (water conditions etc.) ....
....
Equipment required for lesson ....
....
Number of helpers/aides ....   Number of pupils ....
Ability of pupils ....
....
Aims of lesson ....
....

	Activity	**Organisation/Safety**	**Teaching Points**
Explanation			
Entry, Introductory and Warming-Up Activity			
Main Theme Conclusion Contrasting Activity			
Free Practice of Known Skills			
Appraisal of Lesson			

Fig 92   Outline lesson plan 1.

Notes on Outline Lesson Plan 1 (Fig 92)

Values of Preliminary Information

1 To allow the teacher to assess effectively the pupils' potential ability and to select a meaningful and appropriate goal for each individual.
2 To ensure that facilities available for the duration of the lesson have been carefully considered and are suitable.
3 To ensure that the teacher is aware of, and responsible for, the needs of the pupils in the changing room and in handling before and after the swim.

Values of Lesson Plan Format

1 Columns

Activity This column should contain a descriptive word or phrase, indicating the type of activity or practice to be used.
Organisation/Safety In this column should be listed any points relevant to that particular activity or practice, such as the position of swimmers, equipment to be used, the role of aides.
Teaching Points Listed in this column should be those points (which will aid the learning of that skill or activity) which the teacher intends to highlight when teaching the pupils. These should be arranged and worded so that they may be easily recognised and understood.

2 Sections

Explanation This usually takes place on the poolside and the content will depend on the type of lesson planned, the comprehension level of pupils, and the individual style of the teacher. It will obviously vary from lesson to lesson, but where possible the pupils should be aware of the ultimate aim of any lesson. This section of the lesson also brings the class together as a whole.

Entry, Introductory and Warming-Up Activity If necessary, mention how individual pupils should enter the water, particularly if this is to vary from the previous lesson. The introductory activity should warm and loosen the pupils and prepare them for the activities to follow. If possible this should involve the group as a whole, although where necessary individual needs must be catered for.

Main Theme This constitutes the main body of the lesson and should be fulfilling its stated aims. This section may well have to be written out separately for each individual pupil, or for different ability groups. If possible a 'good' demonstration from one particular pupil for the others to copy can be shown, or the skills which each individual has been working on can be drawn into a group activity.

Contrasting Activity This should serve as a contrast to the main body of the lesson, for example in the effort required, skills involved, or emphasis on different muscle groups used. This activity should be particularly steered towards enjoyment and fun and as such will make an excellent contrast.

Free Practice If time is available, this section allows the pupils both freedom and an opportunity to enjoy the water performing activities of their own choice. It should conclude with a quieter, relaxing activity.

Appraisal Should be made at the end of every lesson, indicating activities which were successful, skills which need developing and highlighting problem areas which need to be changed or avoided on future occasions.

LESSON PLANS

Orthodox Lesson Plan

Teacher's Name ....

Preliminary Information:

Aim/Title of Lesson .... Class ....

No. of Pupils .... Age of Pupils .... Water Time .... Pool Conditions ....

Equipment .... Ability of Pupils ....

(Refer to Aim of Lesson)

	Task	Organisation/Safety	Teaching Points
Explanation			
Introductory Activity			
Main Theme			
Contrasting Activity			
Supervised Free Practice			

LESSON EVALUATION:

Introductory Activity
Main Theme
Contrast
ACTION FOR NEXT LESSON:

Evaluation Guidelines:

1 Organisation.
2 Communication.
3 Demonstrations.
4 Relationships.
5 Progression.
6 General effectiveness.

Fig 93   Outline lesson plan 2.

(The preliminary information would need to be included as identified in Lesson Plan 1)

	Objective	Task	Teaching Points or Learning Strategies	Organisation	Appraisal
Introductory Activity					
Main Section of Lesson Development					
Contrasting Activity					

Fig 94   Outline lesson plan 3.

Notes on Outline Lesson Plans 2 and 3 (Figs 93 and 94)

Values of Lesson Plan Format

1 Columns
Objective   This is the immediate aim for the particular section of the lesson. It may be isolated but is usually part of a long-term schedule for a pupil or class.
Task   This may be a practice, or a game type of activity which will help the pupils to achieve the objective.
Teaching Points or Learning Strategies   For each activity these are the key teaching techniques, words or instructions which may be related to the pupils in order to enable them to achieve the objective through the nominated task.
Organisation   Demonstrations; use of equipment; use of aids.
Appraisal   The teacher should assess the values, successes and failures of each section of the lesson for reward and for future assistance in planning.

2 Sections
Introductory Activity   This should attune the pupils to the lesson and the teacher, and prepare them physically and mentally for the activities to follow.
Main Section of the Lesson   This should show a development from the introduction, and should be directly related to the main aim of this particular lesson, which will probably constitute a part of the overall schedule for the pupil.
Contrasting Activity   This provides a conclusion to the lesson, which may need to be a total contrast to the main section and which may involve group work and fun activities or may need to be a calming type of activity. A great deal will depend on the main content.

Appendix 2

Pupil Assessment Sheet

Name of pupil ....

How does disability affect learning? ....
....

Needs of pupil:

Changing room ....
....

Changing room to pool ....
....

Buoyancy aids or support ....
....

Any other ....
....

Initial assessment:

1   Social skills (one to one/group) ....
....

2   Movement control ....
....

3   Water confidence ....
....

4   Water safety:

Buoyancy and balance ....
....

Recovery ....
....

Breathing ....
....

Changing direction ....
....

5   Swimming ability and general comments on strokes ....
....

6   Any other comments ....
....

Progress during practical:

Buoyancy and Balance ....
....

Recovery ....
....

Breathing ....
....

Changing direction ....
....

Evaluation of your success or failure and future aims for pupil ....
....
....

Fig 95   Pupil assessment sheet.

Appendix 3

Water Games

Simple Circle Games

Circles should be small for safety and involvement.

Poison

Players are positioned and moving round in a circle. One or more balls float in the middle of the circle. The players must not touch any ball, imagining it to be poisonous. The aim is to blow a ball towards other players.

Electricity

An imaginary 'current' is passed around a circle of players via their hand squeezes. On receiving a hand squeeze from an adjacent player, that person similarly passes it on to the next player, simultaneously ducking under water.

Number Retrieve

With players in a circle, a ball is thrown into the circle as the teacher shouts a number. The player who has been allocated that number swims or dives to catch the ball and returns to the circle, throwing the ball back to the teacher.

Keep It Up

The aim is to keep a light ball in the air for as long as possible around the circle of players, who repeatedly throw or punch it upwards. This game readily lends itself to simple goal setting, by asking the group to score a given number of airborne shots.

Simple Group Games

Red Letter

One pupil on the opposite side of the pool calls out letters. If the letter occurs in any players' names they may take one step towards the caller. If the caller shouts the 'red letter' (specified beforehand) nobody shall move and the caller aims to catch a player out.

Simon Says

The teacher is 'Simon'. The pupils have to do whatever 'Simon says', and stay still if Simon's name is omitted. The selection of stunts depends on pupil ability, and can be moving or static.

Sharks and Minnows

One player is 'shark' in the middle of the pool. All others are minnows lined up along one side of the pool. 'Shark' shouts 'sharks and minnows' and minnows have to cross to the other side without being caught by shark. Anyone caught stays in the middle and becomes a shark.

What's the Time, Mr Wolf?

'Wolf' stands on one side with his back to the others. Others creep on wolf, calling 'What's the time Mr. Wolf?' As wolf shouts 'dinner time' he turns to try and catch someone for his 'dinner'. (A game useful for promoting involvement.)

149

Traffic Lights

Three corners or sides of the pool are labelled as colours of the traffic lights. The teacher calls a colour and pupils have to move to the appropriate side as quickly as possible. This can also be an elimination game.

Follow the Leader

The leader performs tasks that all can copy. The teacher should ensure that these are suitable for the group.

Musical Games

Played similarly to musical chairs or bumps, the pupils being given a selected task when the music stops. Tasks could be: lie or stand quite still (statue); pick up an object from the pool floor; find a hoop and go inside it; find a ball and throw it up and catch; find a float and balance with it.

Treasure Hunt

Both sinkable and floating objects are scattered in the pool. The aim is to collect as many as possible. Each object is worth different points, those more difficult to retrieve being worth more. Different colours can be used, and pupils told to collect only the 'red' objects, for instance.

Races for Individuals or Pairs

Cork Retrieve

A number of corks are thrown into the pool; whoever collects the most wins.

Wheelbarrow Race

In pairs, one person lies on their front or back horizontally, supported by their partner who stands between their legs and grasps each leg. The race is across the pool, the supporter walking or running and the 'wheelbarrow' with arms extended above the head or using the arms to help propulsion.

Linked Swim

Swimmers link up with two or three others. So linked, they then swim the length of the pool. Through experiment the swimmers choose the most effective method of linking and travelling.

Shadow Swim

In pairs, one person swims underwater, and their partner attempts to 'shadow' the stroke on the surface.

Entry/Stunt/Exit

Swimmers enter the water, execute a designated stunt and then climb out the other side.

Skill Races

Hopping, jumping, running, walking on hands, side stepping, and running backwards. Also blowing objects, 'egg and spoon' using plastic spoons and table tennis balls, throwing and catching balls. Swimmers can use various swimming strokes. Races are across a single width, but the distance can be increased later.

Tag Games

Japanese Tag

A tag game where the catcher touches a certain part of the body of a swimmer in order to catch the person out.

Statue Tag

When a swimmer is touched by the catcher they must stand or float as still as a 'statue'. 'Statues' can be set free by someone else swimming through their legs, or swimming under them.

150

Log Roll Tag

One swimmer sculls or floats like a 'log' in the middle of the pool. The others swim as close as they dare until the log suddenly rolls over and tries to catch as many swimmers as possible before they reach the safety of the side.

Hoop Tag

One swimmer is 'it' and has to catch a replacement. By touching another swimmer the responsibility of being 'it' is transferred. Swimmers are only safe from being caught when within a hoop, holding a ball, or are underwater, according to the task set.

Partner Tag

Two or three catchers initially tag another player. They then must remain linked in pairs as they move to try to tag and so eliminate all other swimmers. Those eliminated can be given a task. (With any tag game, a weak catcher can be aided by helpers.)

Relay Games

Relays take place in shallow or deep water, walking, running, and swimming. Buoyancy aids may be used. They can be run over single or double widths, lengths or longer distances. There should be only four or six swimmers in each team. Players will devise their own relay races with or without equipment. Useful for practising strokes or part strokes.

Over-Under Ball

Swimmers stand one behind the other in a line. Starting at the front, a ball is passed back down over the head, then under the legs and so forth until the end player receives it. That person then moves/swims to the front to start again. Keep this going until the number one is back at the front.

Duck for Ring

Use sinking rings. The rules are then as above except the ring is dropped back over each player's head. The player behind then has to pick it up from the bottom of the pool.

Object Races

Team members swim widths or lengths, having to carry a ball between knees, an object on the tummy, or a ring on the head. Other ideas include: with hands held out of the water, picking an object off the pool floor, going through submerged hoops, swimming whilst propelling a ball.

Tunnel Swim

The teams stand in a long line, their legs apart. The player at the back swims through the team's legs. On reaching the front, the next player swims through from the back.

Dressing Race

Team members swim across, collect an item of clothing, and wear it to swim back. The next player puts that on and also swims to collect a second garment to wear, and so forth.

Obstacle Race

Each member of the team has a different stunt to perform as they swim across, for instance a somersault, a handstand, a log roll, sculling across, taking a ball.

Relay Race

This is performed over a set distance, with 2 or 3 swimmers at either side or end

151

of the pool. Each swimmer makes a designated number of crossings until the end of the relay.

(i)   Start in the water – walk, run, swim on back or front, according to the task set. Next swimmer starts when touched. Finish when all back home.

(ii)   As above, but additionally take a float, push a ball, blow an object, ball between legs, etc.

(iii)   Each swimmer performs a width or length using a different stroke each time they swim, such as breaststroke, side-stroke, backcrawl, butterfly, frontcrawl, and sculling.

(iv)   Using designated part practices, using legs only prone, arms only prone, legs only supine, arms only supine, whole stroke prone, then supine.

(v)   Swimming on the back holding a ball clear of the water.

(vi)   Sculling head leading supine, feet leading supine, head leading prone, rotating.

Ball Games

A variety of ball games can be adapted for the water. Teams should be small. They may be played in shallow water, within the depth of the players, or in deep water (wearing aids if necessary). In deep water, ball games can be very demanding in stamina and the skills to tread water efficiently and to swim quickly with constant change of direction are necessary. Ideally the swimmers themselves should create their own games using the set apparatus available. Ball skills such as throwing and catching, batting, and travelling should be developed individually, then in pairs co-operatively, then in competitive small group situations.

Passing and Catching

Varying distance, type of pass, method of catching, number of participants.

Pass and Catch Relays

A player throws a ball to another swimmer. This can be done in lines, or circles, on the spot, or moving.

Piggy in the Middle

Three swimmers play this game, one standing in the middle attempting to intercept the ball thrown between the other two swimmers. Whoever throws the ball which the 'piggy' intercepts becomes the next piggy.

Partners

This game is played with two teams of two. Each team counts the number of passes it can make with the ball before the other team intercepts.

Volley Ball

A floating net or rope is stretched across the pool. The aim is to get the ball down on to the water on the opposition's side of the net. Three different players must touch the ball on one side before it is sent over the net.

Basketball

A game similar to water polo except small, floating (basketball type) unguarded goals are the targets.

Water Polo

Beginning with three players versus three, with improvised goals and working in a limited area. The game is gradually progressed through many variations, introducing rules as necessary, to a full game.

Appendix 4

Water Exercises

	Body Area Aim	Starting Position Use of Pool	Movement Task	Teaching Point/ Progression
1	General warming.	Standing shoulders under water, move freely in space.	Walk freely, pulling with alternate arms or arms together.	Vary length of step. Vary direction of step. Lift the knee higher. Vary pace.
2	Arms/ shoulders.	Standing, feet astride, shoulders under the water. Use all space around the body.	Arms extended sideways, arms to meet or cross then move to stretch apart.	Vary the point of meeting: at the water surface; under the water. Add hand paddles or floats to increase resistance.
3	Leg/hip.	Standing – one hand supported on the rail.	Lift and lower one leg, with a swinging pendulum action; press against the water.	Exercise with bent leg, then straight leg. Increase the height of the movement. Keep the supporting leg straight. Take away from the rail, and add a hop.
4	Inner thighs, abdomen, hips, waist.	Back to the pool wall, arms spread along the rail. Legs close to the pool floor, or lifted towards the surface.	Scissor the legs: open and close. Bend the knees to chest and stretch out. Twist from waist, side to side, with legs straight or bent.	Increase the size of the movement. Move the legs up and down for a series of movements. Stretch feet as come up, lead with the heels on push away. Keep the upper body firm.
5	Legs, pelvic region, breathing.	Standing, water up to waist or chest.	Sink down and up with a squat position on forward leg, other leg stretched out behind, blow out as submerge.	Begin slowly, increase bounce and submerging. Vary leg position: sideways; forwards. Take sequence to music, increasing the number of repetitions

Body Area Aim	Starting Position Use of Pool	Movement Task	Teaching Point/ Progression
6 General muscle toning.	Floating on the back/front, with float in each hand, or using arm bands.	Lying, contract abdominal/pelvic/ thigh muscles, hold count of 4 and relax. Taking arms/ legs into different directions, hold position then change and hold new position. Rotate the body from front to back. Rotate side to side.	Particularly used in ante/ post-natal groups. Use floats to increase resistance. Leg bent then straight, increase arc of movement. Pendulum swing; with bend and stretch of body, increase the rate and number. Sideways rotation, body stretched.
7 Stamina, general body control.	Free movement using all space in the shallow end.	Jogging. Jumping, two feet, alternate feet. Hopping, lifting free leg high. Movement sequences. Varying pace of movement.	Legs high, vary direction. Encourage submerging and jumping high. Do actions on the spot, then moving. Increase length of time. Use music to accompany. Encourage variety and use of the whole body, with quick pace movements included.
8 Warm down.	Free swimming with or without buoyancy aids, using all the space.	Variety of strokes, sculling and floating.	Accompanied by music, which gradually decreases in tempo.

Glossary

Ambulant A person who is able to move around quite independently of any aids. A non-ambulant person is someone who is bedridden or confined to a wheelchair.

Antenatal Before birth.

Anterior The front of the body.

Aphasia Impaired ability to understand or use language meaningfully.

Aquaphobia Fear of water.

Athetoid A type of cerebral palsy with involuntary slow sinuous writhing movements, especially severe in the hands.

Arth- Word component referring to joints.

Atoxia Failure of muscle co-ordination.

Atrophy Wasted or wasting, i.e. of muscles. A similar effect to dystrophy, as in muscular dystrophy.

Aura In a case of epilepsy this is often a warning sensation.

Autism Inability to form meaningful interpersonal relationships, severe withdrawal.

Back Paddle Swimming on the back, using a crawl-type leg action and sculling arm action.

Bilateral Having two sides.

Body Image Awareness of the position of the body in space and how the body moves.

Catheter A tube used, for example, in cases of urinary incontinence. The tube is used to collect urine in a bag, which is often attached to the leg.

Central Nervous System This consists of the brain and the spinal cord.

Cerebral Pertaining to the brain.

Cognitive Mental process of reasoning, comprehension, memory.

Congenital A condition which materialises at or before birth.

Co-Ordination The interlinking of the movements of different body parts.

Diplegic Paralysis affecting like parts on both sides of the body.

Directionality An understanding and ability to move to the right and left. An extension of laterality.

Dorsi-Flexed Flexion in the ankle joint; the feet turn up.

Downs Syndrome Also known as Mongolism. A specific type of mental retardation, characterised by particular physical features and often a susceptibility to respiratory conditions and a congenital heart condition.

Dystrophy Defective nutrition or development (*see* atrophy). (dys – ,bad, disordered, – trophy, nourish, grow.)

Echolalia An imitative repetition of another person's word or sentence. This is often senseless and without understanding.

Encephalitis Inflammation of the brain.

Enuresis Involuntary discharge of urine.

Flaccid Lack of muscle tone. Floppy and often wasted muscles. A term used to describe a type of paralysis. The opposite of spastic.

Flexibility Quality which permits full range of movement at a joint.

Hemiplegia Paralysis affecting one side of the body (hemi – half).

Hydrotherapy A treatment of physical conditions through the use of exercises and aids. (hydro – water-fluid). Often used in specially-designed and heated pools. Could be described as a kind of physiotherapy in water.

Hyperactivity Abnormally increased activity.

Hypothermia Loss of heat at the vital core of the body.

Incontinence Loss of control of the bladder and/or bowel functions.

Kinaesthetic Sense An awareness of the type, extent and direction of movement. The feel of movement (kine – movement).

Laterality An awareness of the right and left sides of the body, and related movements.

Lesion A break, any pathological or traumatic discontinuity of the use, or loss of function of a part.

Mainstreaming Placement of people with disability into regular educational or community (sport) programmes.

Monoplegic Paralysis affecting one limb of the body.

Multiple Handicaps More than one disability, for example, visual impairment, spastic hemiplegia and mental impairment.

Multi-Sensory Approach A means of communicating used in teaching, whereby all or a variety of the body's senses are used.

Multi-Stroke Beginners attempt different ways of swimming, develop the one which suits them whilst continuing to learn all.

Muscle Tone A state of continuous partial contraction of a muscle as if in readiness for work (tonus).

Neuron A nerve cell.

Neurotic A person with a mild behavioural abnormality; someone who is, however, able to remain in touch with reality and function in society.

Occupational Therapy A therapy which involves purposeful activities as a means of aiding rehabilitation and independence.

Orthopaedic Pertaining to injury, deformity of the skeletal structure (i.e. bones, muscles, joints, tendons), and to the correction of deformities.

Paralysis Loss of muscular control.

Paraplegic Paralysis affecting the lower limbs of the body.

Pathological Pertaining to illness. For example a pathological disability would be poliomyelitis.

Perceptual Awareness The brain being able to interpret sensory input.

Peripheral Around the body, the extremities (peri – around).

Peripheral Nervous System The nerve fibres which link the body's extremities of muscles, organs or senses with the central nervous system.

Peripheral Vision Having sight which extends to the outer extremities and boundaries of vision, but not being able to distinguish images directly ahead.

Physiotherapy The treatment of disability through physical means, using particular manipulative exercises and such properties as heat and water.

Plantar-Flexion Extension at the ankle joint, pointing of the feet.

Post-Natal After birth.

Postural Drainage A treatment of persons with congestion which utilises techniques such as chest massage in conjunction with the patient being positioned slanting head downwards. Used to treat cystic fibrosis.

Prone   On the front, lying face down.

Prosthesis   Artificial appliances, such as arm or leg.

Psychomotor   Interaction of motor behaviour and psychological processes.

Psychotic   Someone with severe personal disturbances, who is out of touch with reality. Psychotic behaviour can be unpredictable, extreme, irrational and unrealistic.

Quadriplegia   Paralysis which affects all four limbs. Sometimes called tetraplegia.

Regression   Returning to a more immature stage of development.

Rehabilitation   Restoring to as near to normal as possible, physically, socially, emotionally and mentally.

Resting Platform   Where there is no means for a person with physical disability to achieve a resting position when swimming, i.e. gripping the rail trough or steps, then it may be necessary to devise a floating platform, possibly with easily accessible handles.

Rigidity   Tenseness of movement, inflexibility.

Self-Help Skills   Social skills involving a person looking after him or herself (dressing, toileting, feeding).

Shower Chair   A wheelchair suitable because of its drainage qualities for use in wet areas and particularly for use under showers.

Spasticity   High muscle tone resulting in less movement or stiff jerky movements and distorted limb positions.

Supine   On the back, lying face upwards.

Tactile   Refers to sense of touch.

Task Analysis   The breaking down of a skill into smaller sequentially-ordered phases and steps.

Trauma   Accident or sudden cause of injury or disability.

Triplegia   Paralysis of three extremities.

Tunnel Vision   A contrary condition to peripheral vision where a visually impaired person only has vision directly in front as if through a 'tunnel'.

Unilateral   Affecting one side.

Warm Down   Gentler movement to allow the body to recover after demanding exercise.

Warm-Up   Initial exercise to prepare the body for strenuous activity.

Further Reading

Swimming Books

Amateur Swimming Association, *The Teaching of Swimming (14th Edition, 1987)*.
American Red Cross, *Adapted Aquatics* (Doubleday & Co., 1977).
Association of Swimming Therapy, *Swimming for the Disabled* (A & C Black, 1981).
Chamberlain, J., Elkington, H., *Synchronised Swimming* (David & Charles, 1986).
Corlett, G., *Swimming Teaching, Theory and Practice* (Kay & Ward, 1980).
Cross, R., (ed.) *ASA Guide to Better Swimming* (Pan Books, 1987).
Elkington, H., *Swimming – A Handbook for Teachers* (Cambridge University Press, 1978).
Gray, J., *Synchronised Swimming* (J.F.B. Camberley, 1986).
Grimes, D., Krasevec, J., *Hydrorobics* (Leisure Press, 1984).
Verrier, J., *Swimming* (Crowood Press, 1985).

Sport, Physical Education and Disabilities

Brown, A., *Active Games for Children with Movement Problems* (Harper & Row, 1987).
Brown, A., (ed.) *Adapted Physical Activities* (Jenny Lee Publishing, 1984).
De Pauw, K., Seaman, J., *The New Adapted Physical Education* (Mayfield Publishing, 1982).
Groves, L., (ed.) *Physical Education for Children with Special Needs* (Cambridge University Press, 1979).
Male, J., Thompson, C., *The Educational Implications of Disability* (Jason Press, 1985).
Price, R.J., *Physical Education and the Physically Handicapped Child* (Lepus Books, 1980).

Pamphlets

Available from the Co-ordinating Committee on Swimming for the Disabled, all published by The Sports Council (1987).

Forming a Club.
Lifting and Handling.
Facilities.
Medical Consideration.
Swimming and Epilepsy.
Classification Systems in Competitive Swimming.

Index